What others are sayin

"Bart has written a successful, inspirati
zine's website, www.hotelsmag.com, for several years now. He has
taught his blog readers about how to use everyday life experiences to
create further successes in their professional lives, offered ideas on how
to turn negative situations into positives, and how to work best with
and motivate contemporaries and colleagues. He has been loyal to his
blog, always creative and humble throughout. HOTELS has been lucky
to have him contribute his ideas and spirit of good to its readers."

-Jeff Weinstein, Editor In Chief, HOTELS magazine

"I have known Bart for over 10 years and have been struck not only by
his success in sales and marketing, but in his innate ability to motivate
and inspire those around him. I've followed his various writings online
and have been so impressed. I have found his passion, enthusiasm and
conviction to be contagious. He is an outstanding leader and tremendous speaker, writer and visionary."

-Dan Cole, Vice President, Business Development,
Consumer Electronics Association

"Bart Berkey served as keynote speaker for the School of Hospitality
Management's Recognition Ceremony. His presentation style was very
engaging, and the content of his remarks was right on target for the
audience; great career and life suggestions for the graduates, excellent
anecdotes and examples to make the points, and a good mix of humor.
Overall, great takeaways and a memorable presentation."

-Dr. Bart Bartlett, Professor-In-Charge Undergraduate Program,
HRIM, Pennsylvania State University

"Bart has the experience, skills and proven track record to help you achieve
your highest level of results. With his unique blend of creativity and com-
passion, he will help you to find your inner desires and the passion, focus
and goals needed to achieve the results you thought were impossible. Bart
has been instrumental to me and the members of my team."

-Doug Baarman, Senior Vice President, Conference Direct

MOST PEOPLE DON'T
(And Why You Should)

Bart Berkey

First published by Dog Ear Publishing
4010 W. 86th Street, Ste H
Indianapolis, IN 46268
www.dogearpublishing.net

ISBN: 978-1-4575-2437-0

This book is printed on acid-free paper.

Printed in the United States of America

Dedication

This book is dedicated to my wife Terri, who has raised my standard *for* living. To my son Max and daughter Alexa, who have allowed my wife and me to experience unconditional love. To my parents Bill and Ellie, who not only created me, but who also support me in all of my choices to find happiness. To my sisters, who through their own unique ways have set examples for me to follow. To my relatives, friends, and colleagues who – through their interactions and experiences – have allowed me to improve my own life. And to my current employer, who created an environment where I can truly be myself and be happy.

Introduction

Do you have any memories as a child that impacted your life? I remember very clearly in third grade, during recess, my classmates and I were preparing to play a game of kickball. I was one of the captains and could choose my team. My kickball experience during first and second grades taught me a lot. I knew the kids who could run fast, catch well and kick the farthest. I also knew which kids weren't as athletic and kept score on the pavement. To this day, I still remember seeing the disappointment on the faces of a few kids who were never selected to play. As captain, I decided I would make a difference during this one-hour break after lunch.

My first choice was Betsy, a red-haired, pink-faced classmate who was not the most physically fit. My second was Everett, who had been mocked ever since his bathroom accident in first grade. While I can't remember everyone's names, I do remember that my choices bewildered the other team's captain, the kids and even the teachers. But this day wasn't about winning. It was about being kind toward others. And, to this day, my mother often reminds me of my benevolence when I hear her telling a story that never seems to get old.

I continue to have a passion toward others and an innate desire to make everyone feel comfortable. That's why it was a natural fit for me to pursue a career in the hospitality business. While I enjoyed the liberal arts, the hotel world gave me a chance to serve others and actually make a living. Fast forward more than 20 years and I became the first sales and marketing recruiter for a particular luxury hotel company. I was using my perception skills on a daily basis as I sought to recommend and hire only the "best of the best" for our open jobs. During my interviews, I made sure candidates were comfortable and left the interview feeling good about the conversation and their accomplishments regardless of their likelihood of landing the job. This position also allowed me to observe the tendencies and characteristics of the best candidates to see what made them shine.

During my time as a recruiter, I spoke to more than 1,000 candidates. However, only a small portion actually impressed me enough to be recommended for the job. Those who passed the initial stage all came prepared. The best candidates took notes, asked relevant questions, researched the position and the company, and followed up appropriately and timely. I was curious why everyone didn't behave the same way. Suddenly, it became very clear that a common theme existed among those candidates who did *not* leave a favorable impression. They simply "didn't" while the best candidates "did." The "best" used their summer breaks to complete internships instead of vacationing. The "best" listed their accomplishments on their resumes rather than their job duties. The "best" followed up not only with an e-mail, but a handwritten note and a phone call. The "best" had references send me messages before I even asked for them. I called this "MPD" or "Most People Don't." Most people did not come prepared, did not follow up and did not say "thank you." When I noticed this behavior in a professional setting, I immediately began to see it in all aspects of human interaction.

"I'll send you the photos I took."

"I'll call you so we can have lunch."

"I'll volunteer my time to help others."

There are many things people don't do in life. If you're able to "do" even a fraction of things others aren't doing, you will automatically differentiate yourself from the crowd. If you're interested in rising above the rest and being exceptional when everyone else is adequate, please keep reading. This easy-to-remember philosophy can help you professionally when you're trying to make an impression, obtain a sale or finish a project. This mantra can also help you personally by showing distinct efforts toward enhancing a relationship or even expanding a friendship.

"MPD" show kindness toward others.

"MPD" help others while traveling.

"MPD" say thank you.

On your next trip, hold the door open for another person. Help a mother who is traveling by herself with three small children. Lift a bag into the overhead bin for an elderly person. Say "thank you" to the captain who landed you safely in another city. Years ago, I was asked to write for a blog for "HOTELS" online magazine (www.hotelsmag.com). I was encouraged to share real-life stories with readers on how my experiences could promote new ideas, instill motivation and provide inspiration. This book is an aggregation of the most popular blog postings (out of more than 500 articles) that have been tailored to appeal not only to hospitality professionals, but also to anyone looking to improve themselves. I've received comments from students, professors, entrepreneurs, sales people and mothers. I've been heard as far as India, where the owner of a juice bar reads my messages weekly to his employees during staff meetings. Professors in Pennsylvania have been using my stories for group projects, and mothers in Santa Monica, California gather during their monthly book club to gain inspiration.

I'm hopeful my unique perspective will motivate others to look at different ways of approaching life. I'm hopeful that by "doing", you will elevate your self worth, the value of your uniqueness, and improve how others perceive you. I'm hopeful that by "doing" you can differentiate yourself from others to gain greater opportunities, deeper friendships, more solid relationships and increased happiness.

May you become a "PTD" (Person That Does) and enjoy life to its fullest!

Fear Of Missing Something Awesome (FOMSA)

During a recent trip to Baltimore, I explored the Little Italy neighborhood and watched a game of Bocce ball being played by people of all ages. I stopped in a local Italian deli (Isabella's) afterwards and saw some of the teams enjoying wood-fired pizza.

I was intrigued to see older experts enjoying the game with younger, less experienced couples. I asked a young couple what inspired them to play and the wife told me it's a great way to socialize. The husband simply replied, "FOMSA." Was that some type of text abbreviation? The man said it stood for "Fear of Missing Something Awesome" and explained how he couldn't live without the sport. In other words, he told me he tries not to miss out on anything fun, whether it's Bocce ball in Baltimore or a game of Sunday flag football with his buddies. His friends quickly learned about "FOMSA" and started calling him at odd hours just to see if he wanted to do just about anything fun at any time.

I walked away from that summer night in Baltimore with a new appreciation for new things and living life to the fullest. Yes, we all work tremendously hard. And while it might be difficult to muster up enough energy for fun and exploration after a long day, remember "FOMSA" and the inspirational lyrics of Bon Jovi: "Live when I'm alive, sleep when I'm dead."

MPD: Accept every invitation to try
something new.

My Dog's Feet Smell Like Fritos

It may sound crazy but take a moment to smell a dog's feet. You'll discover they smell like corn chips. What does this have to do with your professional career or personal happiness?

Google the question "why do my dog's feet smell like Fritos?" and you'll find more than 16,000 references to this topic. Are you informed and interesting as a salesperson or as a college candidate? Do you read the paper and listen to the news? Can you have a conversation with anyone? Perhaps the correlation between Fritos and dog feet may never come up the next time you're entertaining a client or meeting a new boss. Then again, if they have a dog, you never know.

The first time I entertained a customer was in Pittsburgh in 1989. I had a top representative from the United Steel Workers Association join me for a tour of my hotel. We wrapped up the tour a bit early (11:15 a.m.) and proceeded to the hotel's restaurant for a late breakfast.

The gentleman was in his early 70's and accustomed to ordering a Bloody Mary with just about every meal. Keep in mind my mentor taught me to be a chameleon with my clients. He ordered alcohol and I knew I needed to the same. I wasn't a vodka drinker at the time so I politely requested a beer to go along with my eggs and toast.

MPD: Acquire the skills to be informed and interesting.

What Is Your Solution?

It's time to think creatively and compare your thought process with the management team of a well-known country or health club.

Here's the scenario:

- This particular exercise facility usually provides bottled water
- The bottled water wasn't available this week. Perhaps the club missed a shipment or forgot to place an order.
- The cardio room only provides access to the ladies locker room (with sink and showers). The main locker room is located in a separate building.
- About 25 people exercise here daily between 6 a.m. and 9 a.m.
- The filtered water machine has been out of service for the last year
- The coffee machine has been out of service equally as long

What would you do to satisfy these members? Some suggestions I received:

- Provide a vending machine with bottled water for a minimal price
- Offer reusable, eco-friendly water containers and have a filtered water system available
- Fill up a large container with water, ice and sliced fruit to create an inexpensive beverage
- Don't purchase any water bottles until the shipment arrives

The theme here is to properly communicate the problem to guests and provide temporary solutions. By brainstorming with others, new solutions can be created that one individual by themselves wouldn't be able to produce.

MPD: Propose solutions instead of excuses.

Leadership Lessons Learned On The Racetrack

I used to own a 1992 Toyota Supra Twin Turbo with 320 horsepower that would rocket to 60 mph in less than five seconds. I purchased the car when I was living in California and a friend suggested I take it to Summit Point Motorsports Park in West Virginia. The instructors there taught me many valuable lessons about safe driving, when to brake, how to accelerate and the proper "lines" to take. One message stood out above the others. "The farther you look ahead on the track, the faster you will be able to go."

Great leaders are visionaries who look at today, tomorrow, next week, next month and next year. Tactical leaders look at what needs to be done today. Strategic leaders look into the future to map out plans that will help meet future goals.

On the track I hit a top speed of 120 mph on the straightaway but only reached 85 mph on the curves and bends. I would have known to slow down had I looked ahead for the next turn. Soon enough, I increased my speed simply by anticipating my next move.

In business (and in life) the farther out you're able to look, the faster you'll be able to go. If you can save for retirement now and establish a college fund for your children, you can also start working on your marketing plan for next year.

MPD: Look farther ahead to go faster.

The Punctual Porsche

It doesn't matter how early I arrive into our office building or how late I leave. I always see the same Porsche parked in the garage within two or three spots from my car. This sports car probably costs about $90,000, which is more than triple the price of my used 2005 Saab. Eight years ago, I encountered the same situation with a similar Porsche (different year and color) while I was working for a different company. It was always there before everyone arrived and the last to leave.

I've never met the owners of these cars but would like to learn a few things about them:

- Is it worth it? Do they enjoy working more than everyone else?
- Are the privileges of making enough money to afford such a car worth the increased responsibilities and commitment?

You should ask yourself:

- Is it worth it? Do you enjoy doing what you're doing?
- Are the privileges, benefits and pay worth your commitment?

I'm fortunate enough to be working for an outstanding organization with an incredible group of people. I would always like to make more money. However, I work hard not for the Porsche I don't have but for the job I love. In that sense I'm truly wealthy!

MPD: Work for enjoyment and self-worth.

Finding Pennies And Remembering Bubby

Several years ago we lost a very special lady who battled lung cancer for nine years. My mother-in-law, Bubby, was always up for everything and anything. She was positive and enjoyed life to the fullest. It has been hard to understand why such a positive person who brought happiness to so many people is no longer with us. During the holidays it's more quiet than usual without her. We miss her brisket, her laugh, her energy and her love.

We made many decisions about her health over the years and felt good about our choices. Every year we think about Bubby and what's truly important in life. Sometimes the holidays bring excess (food, gifts, beverages, etc.). And sometimes this excess distracts us from realizing how much we love our family and our friends.

As a result, we've resolved to:
- Eliminate the clutter (in our offices, on your computers, in our homes)
- Focus on what's important (health, family and happiness)
- Enjoy what we do every day (if not, make plans to change what we do)
- Communicate openly and honestly (there's no resolution in silence)

Bubby was always the first to pick up the check at dinner, to bring special gifts for the kids, to alter her schedule to help others. She was the first to reach into her purse and give pennies to the kids to toss into the "wishing" fountains. These days we're reminded of her when we find pennies in the most unusual places.

It's Bubby's way of reminding us of what's important.

MPD: Remember what's important.

Bart Berkey

Friends Longer Than Colleagues

I recently received an e-mail from a candidate who I spoke to more than three years ago when I was a recruiter. "I just wanted to send you a quick and sincere 'hello.' I hope you remember me — you and I had a career chat a while back. I wanted to reconnect and tell you how much I appreciate your kindness to a stranger. Thank you again for your advice and time, and for your mentoring spirit," she wrote.

I spoke with more than 1,000 candidates during my recruiting days and I don't fully recall this conversation. I'm sure I would remember by taking another look at her resume. Nevertheless, I'm pleased I was able to positively impact someone's life in a short amount of time.

I believe you should always help others and give good career advice (especially to coworkers) because you can be friends longer than you may be colleagues. I once interviewed a gentleman for a job at an Internet startup company (unfortunately, we couldn't afford his salary) who ended up hiring me when he became the president of a CVB.

"Our relationships with others are like bridges that take us from one place to another; when we 'burn our bridges' we destroy our relationships and make it difficult to go back." – goenglish.com

How have you shared career kindness with someone recently?

Has the effort repaid you in some form?

MPD: Maintain good relationships with others.

Gift-Wrapped Groceries

If you grew up during the 1980s chances are you remember celebrating holidays and birthdays with plenty of gifts. Every year my mother would wrap containers of peanuts, toothpaste, mouthwash and socks to create the illusion of lots of loot under the Christmas tree. Of course, she would also throw the occasional "boom box" or highly sought Mattel football game into the mix.

Parents during that bygone era could usually get away with a relatively inexpensive holiday (especially given the propensity to wrap grocery items). Now, a newly released Nintendo Wii game costs at least $49. Buy four games and you're into the spirit an easy $200. Keep in mind these small gifts amount to barely two inches stacked under the tree.

Are the holidays about quantity or quality, memories, food or friends?

In the movie "Morning Glory," a romantic comedy starring Rachel McAdams, Harrison Ford and Diane Keaton (not all romantically linked), McAdams plays the part of a TV producer for a morning television program. The morning show contains many dysfunctional characters and was struggling to stay on the air. (SPOILER ALERT: McAdams eventually turns down a pristine job on the "Today" show because she was happy staying with her hard-working colleagues and friends).

We all work hard. Take the time to celebrate your successes with your teammates.

Time may not be as abundant as wrapped toiletry items, but we can enjoy the quality of every moment with family and friends.

MPD: Enjoy quality time with family and friends.

Handling Disappointment; "America's Got Talent"

Imagine you are an 11-year-old girl who loves to sing. You wake up early every day and put on your headphones to belt out a few lyrics before school. You teach yourself how to play the piano. You print out the lyrics and memorize your favorite songs. You sing at your elementary school's talent show. You create your own YouTube channel and upload a new song every day.

I'm sure many of you would love to have such passion for a hobby. My daughter had the opportunity to audition for "America's Got Talent" in Charlotte, North Carolina. She entered a convention center filled with thousands of hopeful entertainers and immediately embraced the challenge. When the time came to sing a few lines in a small room with a producer and four other applicants, she stood tall and gave it her best shot.

This was in January and they told her finalists would be announced in March. My daughter woke up early every day in March to check the website for updates. I told her how proud I was of her and that I was sorry nothing had been announced. She simply smiled and sang another song. She finally saw that she didn't advance to the next round for the show.

She said it was "okay" and asked if she could make another video of a new song. I learned from my wife that she sent this video to "The Ellen DeGeneres Show."

Things don't always go as planned in sales but it's up to us to determine how we react. Thank you to my daughter, Alexa, for teaching me how to handle disappointment and persevere like a superstar.

MPD: Grow stronger from disappointment.

My Lifeguard Texts

The lifeguards at our neighborhood pool last summer choose to send text messages to their friends instead of watching people swim! I started to notice this near the end of the season. I surmised that these temporary workers were getting tired, but I couldn't lose sight of the fact that a lifeguard's job is to truly "guard a person's life" by paying attention.

Over at the snack shop, I noticed that the workers no longer stood up when customers came into the restaurant. I even caught a cook sitting on the floor!

Suddenly, after a few raindrops, the lifeguards would close the pool (and be allowed to go home).

The kitchen workers shut off the grill at 6:50 p.m. instead of 7 p.m. and refused to open for a hungry kid who just wanted a grilled cheese sandwich.

Keep up the momentum.

A family who arrives at a pool late in the day deserves to have as much fun as a family who arrives when the gates open. A person should be able to grab a cookie or another dessert on a buffet at 2:10 p.m. when they were just seated at 1:30 p.m.

Keep up the momentum.

How is your team doing with momentum? Are your team members tired and falling behind? Are they still putting forth the effort required to make their goals?

What are you doing to keep them lively, motivated and productive? Is this a generational issue? Do they need to be supported, reprimanded or held accountable? Do you need support? Do you need to be disciplined or managed?

MPD: Maintain consistent efforts regardless of your own energy level.

Bart Berkey

NASCAR Driver's Greatest Fear

If you were a professional race car driver and had to navigate the track at speeds upwards of 200 mph (322 km/h), what would be your greatest fear?

I would be afraid of crashing and injuring myself.

ESPN interviewed drivers after Dale Earnhardt Jr. decided (based on his doctor's recommendation) to sit out two races due to concussions he sustained on the track. Each competitor mentioned the same thing and said staying out of the race car is every driver's greatest fear.

Perhaps it's the fear of losing traction and momentum (this injury stopped Earnhardt's streak of 461 consecutive starts), fear of losing the coveted spot in a sponsored car (and essentially one's job), or fear of not doing what drivers love.

I once met a saleswoman who was so worried about losing her job she neglected to *do* her job. The fear created paralysis and lead her to second guess every decision. Have confidence in your ability, your product and your efforts! Make the extra phone call to ensure your success.

What's your greatest fear in your current position? Is it not being able to sell? Not having the freedom to make decisions? Not making your goal and losing your job?

What are you doing to overcome this challenge?

MPD: Focus on winning once you're in the game and fight diligently to keep playing.

The Appreciation Advantage

A mother once told me that her nine-month-old baby's favorite gift was the wrapping paper on his presents. In hindsight, she could've saved herself a lot of effort and money.

My team recently had the opportunity to plan several customer events. One of our largest was a sponsored golf tournament with a day of culinary gluttony. We had 50 of our top clients combined with our hotel partners. And the bill wasn't cheap. Four months later, no one on our team received a "thank you" via e-mail, a phone call or even a letter from the prestigious country club.

We subsequently coordinated a small event for 12 of our top customers that cost a lot less than the golf tournament. We received an e-mail from the owner of the venue the next day thanking us for the business and asking for any feedback. It was a simple and gracious gesture that took a matter of seconds. We are now customers for life.

Do people know how much you appreciate their thoughtfulness? Do your customers know how much you appreciate their loyalty and do you illustrate it throughout the year? If you take the time to say "thank you" and your competition doesn't, who wins? I still hold onto notes from candidates I interviewed years ago since they were the ones who truly stood out from the crowd!

MPD: Say thank you as many times
as it takes.

Bart Berkey

The Importance Of Asking Questions

I had the opportunity to attend a trade show event one year that paired meeting planners with suppliers who were there to sell their goods and services. I came across a saleswoman from a promotional product company who was busy promoting her items. She was eloquent, confident and organized in her approach, and even used an iPad to show samples of her product. I listened to her presentation and was initially impressed... until I kept watching.

She spent the first 15 minutes (of a 20-minute appointment) explaining her passion and enthusiasm for her product and barely gave the client a chance to speak. Only when one customer finally had a chance to talk did she learn that he had a relative in the same industry. Any purchases of giveaway items would most likely be made with his cousin.

What if this saleswoman had started the conversation by asking questions? "Can you tell me about which promotional product company you currently use and why?" This could have saved everyone time and money.

Have you seen a salesperson promoting a "kids program" to a customer whose kids are in college? Do you sell steak to a vegetarian group? Would you accept a job without knowing the pay and expectations? Would you promote your refurbished racquetball court to a group of disabled veterans?

MPD: Ask questions and stop talking.

Managing The "We Are Busy" Message

As occupancy levels and room rates rise with increased confidence in the economy, it becomes even more important to manage the perception of being busy. It's all in the delivery. When a restaurant is booked it's critically important how you handle any additional reservation requests. You want customers to call again when you have availability.

Sales people need to be careful and recognize the value of any business opportunities. Even though each lead may not be perfect, it's up to the creativity and ingenuity of the sales professional to provide options and solutions.

Rates need to increase for various reasons: to pay increasing utility bills and other operational costs; to meet ownership commitments on investments; to renovate and improve a physical product; to enhance service levels and offerings; and to allow for organizational expansion and development.

Sales professionals can't offer emotional reasons why a loyal, repeat customer has to pay 20 percent more than in previous years. They need to show the client the reasons why rate increases are sometimes required to retain their valued business. Keep in mind you can always offer solutions such as a different set of dates or a new pattern that would allow for a lower rate increase. Perhaps the client can offer additional food and beverage needs that would create additional revenue for the hotel and a win-win scenario for both parties.

Any message can be delivered with care and tact. Even the traditional "no vacancy" signs have the option to include "sorry" in the beginning. Perhaps even more sensitive placards can be created in the future such as: "While we really appreciate your interest in staying with us, we unfortunately don't have rooms for tonight. We would be happy to accommodate you tomorrow evening or can suggest another hotel for tonight."

Too long for a sign?

MPD: Deliver the impression of busyness delicately.

When You Don't Respond

I learned a valuable lesson over the past year involving e-mail etiquette. Many of us receive as many as 200 e-mails a day and we all know how challenging it can be to respond to each and every message.

A colleague of mine solved this problem in a simple way. When she receives a message she responds with a quick "thanks" or "received." If the message includes a question she doesn't have time to answer, she acknowledges receiving the message and says she will respond soon. In this case senders don't have to worry that their messages are going unread.

When you don't respond the sender may conclude that you never took the time to open the e-mail.

The same holds true for authors who don't receive feedback on their books. When I don't receive any messages I assume my ideas aren't being read. Post a message on my twitter account @bartberkey to prove me wrong!

MPD: Respond to every message.

You're Getting Dressed Anyway

You might as well look GREAT!

Did you bypass one of your favorite shirts this morning because you're not going to see a customer? Did you put on more comfortable shoes that were a little dusty because you need to walk to a sales appointment? Each day there are certain things we need to do to get ready for work. One of these is to get dressed.

Unfortunately, I can't offer advice for the ladies, however, I can provide some suggestions I've received in the past from "fashion mentors":

- Polish your shoes as often as necessary
- Wear a white t-shirt under a white dress shirt to make it look even brighter
- Consider using pocket squares to enhance your appearance
- Get your hair cut often. In between cuts, ensure that you trim any neck hair with a razor.
- Be neatly shaved
- Ensure that your suit fits you and is tailored properly
- Wear socks that stay up and match
- Iron wrinkled ties

Is it cooler to have a five o'clock shadow for an interview than to have a job?

MPD: Dress each day like you are interviewing for a new job.

Lessons From A Sushi Server

Do you like sushi? Our family enjoys Japanese food because it offers enough variety to please everyone. It's also a welcomed diversion from the typical kid's menu of chicken fingers and fries. However, I always find myself dealing with impatient servers who don't want to take the time to please their customers.

Restaurant servers are supposed to be experts on the menu and the cuisine. Many courageous diners still want to learn and experiment by trying new dishes. Of course, I understand there may be times of frustration when customers order customized sushi (inside out, cut in eight pieces, no roe and mayo on the side). How many times has your California roll arrived with those lovely orange eggs but caviar is the last thing you want on your sushi?

My family and I had the best sushi experience in Sarasota, Florida thanks to a particular server. She asked us questions and wanted to know what we really liked. She offered suggestions and welcomed our special requests. She repeated the order to ensure accuracy. She was pleasant and didn't make us feel uncomfortable. She thanked us for our business and told us to ask for her upon our return.

Do we make others feel comfortable or make them feel inferior? Do we use terms or acronyms that they may not understand? Do we know what they truly want based on our questions? Are we pleasant and do we thank them for their business? The sushi may not be memorable but we'll never forget the interaction with our superior server.

MPD: Make others feel comfortable.

No Reason To Look Elsewhere

We held a VIP client event earlier this year at a wine venue in New York City's Tribeca neighborhood. This was the third consecutive year we selected this location only because the staff and owner always create an exceptional experience. Their team consistently delivers and raises the bar internally to challenge themselves. We typically prefer to change locations and introduce our guests to new places. However, each year we find ourselves in the same spot in New York City.

Customer loyalty will only go so far when you make mistakes. Forgiveness may be offered once or twice, but after several mishaps your clients may begin to look elsewhere.

However, your customers may consider staying with you if their problems are handled quickly, sincerely and effectively. Treat them with kindness and show appreciation and you'll retain their loyalty for a lifetime! The same approach will work with personal relationships too. Don't give your friend or partner a reason to look elsewhere for friendship, companionship or love.

Are you consistently delivering for your customers? When you don't (as we are all human), how are you handling the mistakes? Are you creating a situation where you give your clients no reason to look elsewhere?

MPD: Create situations in which losing a customer is unacceptable and impossible.

Service That Shocked Me

I travel frequently and enjoy seeing new cities and meeting interesting people. My job also allows me to see a side of our industry I might not be able to see if I was confined to an office. One Sunday night, my flight was leaving from Washington Dulles to go to New York City's Kennedy Airport.

I saw three baggage employees waving goodbye to the plane as it backed away from the gate. I felt good and waved back even though I knew the gesture wasn't directed at me. It reminded me of the times when non-ticketed passengers could walk their family members up to the gate and wave through the windows.

This was such a simple gesture and the employees seemed to be sincere. I was honestly touched by their efforts. It's nice to be shocked by great service for a change.

MPD: Provide exceptional service even when it's not expected.

Sweat The Small Stuff Please

You may have heard the phrase "don't sweat the small stuff" but I'm imploring you to please and respectfully disobey. This is what happens when you ignore the small details:

A sign on a coffee machine in my gym has read "temporarily out of order" for the last 18 months. I see it everyday when I exercise and it continues to bother me.

What happens when we miss the small details?

Friends of ours just returned from vacation. They spent an extra $250 per day to rent a private poolside cabana. The staff misspelled their family name on the reservation sign. Despite good service and refreshing daiquiris, this one simple mistake dampened the experience and irritated them every time they returned from the pool back to their shaded canopy.

The other evening my family and I were enjoying a buffet at a restaurant. As I prepared to move onto my entrée, I set my salad dish to the side. I waited five minutes for the server to clear the dish and then placed it on a nearby clean table to simply get it out of the way. We then counted 12 servers and two managers who passed by the dirty plate for ten minutes and 48 seconds (yes, I timed it).

What small details have you noticed in your life that could be easily remedied?

For professionals, it may be as simple as double-checking the spelling of a customer's name. For students, it may be double-checking a resume or job application. For years I've been hiding coins in areas that should be cleaned just to see how long they remain untouched. A well-known kitchen supply store left my penny alone for almost ten years.

MPD: Be concerned about the small details.

The One Thing And Yearly Resolutions

Newspapers, television and social media all use the month of December to recap major news stories that occurred during the year. A quick glance of *USA Today* reveals the passing of famous celebrities and entertainers. The articles also highlight the year's greatest sports moments as well as major business achievements.

What is the "one thing" you would like to remember about this past year? Was it meeting your goal of responding to all e-mails within 20 seconds?

Were you proud of working every weekend since January to stay ahead of the competition even though you missed most of your kid's soccer games?

When all is said and done you've gone to sleep and awoken 365 times in a year. What is the "one thing" that makes you the most proud? If you're having difficulty identifying this single task perhaps you should pause for additional reflection.

Now is your chance to start fresh before you make a decision that may not make you proud. If you want to become healthier next year, now is the time to decide and commit before you eat another cupcake or miss another morning walk.

MPD: Start today to improve your life.

Using The Telephone For Talking

A friend of mine was complaining about how difficult it had become to reach people on the phone. He also mentioned that competitors were bombarding his clients trying to win their business.

How do you feel when you get a solicitation call at home that interrupts your dinner? You probably feel even more annoyed when the caller promotes something that doesn't interest you. How do you react when you get an unsolicited e-mail? You have more control over e-mail messages and junk mail since you can easily hit the delete button or pitch the paper into a recycle bin. A phone ringing in the middle of dinner is a bit more intrusive but you always have the option not to answer.

How can you be respectful toward clients while inquiring about their needs? One client told me "I appreciate that you're doing your job as a salesperson, but don't call and ask me if I have a meeting in Pittsburgh without doing enough research to know we've never met on the East Coast." How can you establish a connection anytime you use the phone to call a colleague, a potential employer or even a prospective date?

Tip #1: Do your research. Know the needs of the person you're calling. Identify those customers who might have a need (perhaps lost business accounts or retired accounts that had prior business in your area).

Tip #2: Be respectful. It's important during a cold call to make a brief introduction and then ask if it's a convenient time to speak. If not, ask to schedule a time when you may call back. Send an e-mail with your intentions and ask for a time (offering several dates and times) to chat.

Tip #3: Be yourself. Practice your calls so you don't sound like a salesperson. Show the client that you're a real person within the first ten seconds by avoiding sales jargon. "How are you today?" seems to be an overly used introduction to get people talking. Avoid it and be original. "This is Bart with XYZ. I know you get many calls from companies looking for business. I did some research and called you because (...you met with us before, you've used our competitors before, you've been in our city before) and I simply have three questions to ask you if it's a good time to speak?"

This approach will help you anytime you use your telephone for talking and not just texting!

MPD: Have a plan before you use
the phone.

Where Do Your Employees Park?

Do your employees park in front of your building or do they park in the corner of the lot to reserve the best spots for customers?

Do you allow them to smoke in front of your business and alienate paying customers? How do you weigh the prospect of inconveniencing your employees against the needs of your clients?

I was on an empty domestic flight during a business trip. My colleague got upgraded to first class and felt guilty since I was still in economy. There were plenty of first class seats available but my status didn't earn me an upgrade this time around. I was surprised to see an "off the clock" uniformed flight attendant board at the last minute and walk directly to a first class seat. It was apparent she was going to be well taken care of by her co-workers and her company.

Was this the right thing to do for an employee who was clearly dressed as an employee? I believe the way companies treat their employees is critically important to an organization's overall success. But this time something seemed wrong.

In the hotel business employees can take off their name badges and easily blend into the crowd. Guests wouldn't know if an employee had the best suite or the worst room. I've also seen servers and chefs eat in restaurants unbeknownst to customers.

Where will your employees park next week?

MPD: Treat employees with respect but not at the expense of customers.

Three Qualities Needed To Be Great

I've had the opportunity to interview hundreds of people, and I've kept track of the qualities that make people successful regardless of their positions or experience.

1. Response time
2. Follow up
3. Persistence

Imagine you're pursuing the love of your life and that person calls and leaves you a message. You can wait, play hard to get, and hope he or she doesn't schedule a date with someone else. Or you can call the person back <u>QUICKLY</u> and start the relationship you always wanted. The result is that the other person feels wanted and special.

Isn't this how we should make our customers feel?

When you like a person on the first date you <u>FOLLOW UP</u> and ask he or she out on a second date. If the person misses your message you <u>PERSIST</u> and place another call. This scenario is very direct and avoids game playing. Are you playing games these days in business?

1. Be the first to call a customer or a potential employer back
2. Ensure they have what they need and that you've met their needs
3. Keep calling until you reach an agreement (and continue the relationship once the deal is done)

Your job title might not contain the word "sales." However, we're all selling by talking positively and promoting our schools, our companies and ourselves.

MPD: Follow up quickly and relentlessly.

Bart Berkey

Seven Steps To Getting A Job

The competition for jobs has become fierce. The example below comes from the hotel industry but the strategy applies to anyone looking for a job.

When I was a recruiter I would get calls from candidates in the financial industry who wanted to transfer their skills to the hotel world. The conversation would usually end abruptly whenever I asked about salary expectations. The hospitality business isn't difficult to learn, but it's an easier match for someone who has general knowledge of hotels and service. College hospitality students who studied the vocabulary and theories always have a good chance of landing a job.

I once received a call from someone who was a salesperson for a luxury aircraft company. His base salary was $250,000 and his bonus potential was equal to his base. He thought selling luxury to an aircraft customer would be similar to selling luxury to hotel guests. I quickly pointed out that the main difference would be the price of the product ($40 million for a plane versus $400 for a guestroom) and that the starting salary for a hotel salesperson would be significantly less.

How can someone outside the industry go about getting a hotel sales job? How can someone looking for a new challenge obtain a new position? I've seen meeting planners easily assume hotel sales positions. Here are a few suggestions for professionals who currently don't have industry experience and for college students who want to enter into the hospitality sales world:

1. Identify the top six hotels (or other top companies you'd like to consider). Use a meeting planner search engine like Cvent or StarCite to find the properties.
2. Call the general phone number to acquire the name and contact information for the general manager and the director of sales & marketing (or the hiring manager).
3. Send an e-mail with a request for a brief "fact finding" meeting to learn and understand their perspectives on their industry. This will appeal to the ego side for many and most people like to share their success stories with others. This will be easiest for a college student whose sole purpose is to learn and develop. Offer to bring them their favorite coffee drink and commit to no more than 15 minutes for the meeting.
4. Follow up with a phone message in three days if there's no response to your initial e-mail

5. After the initial meeting propose to volunteer your time (based on your area's labor laws). Mention that you want to break into the industry and realize it can be difficult to make the leap without experience. Suggest a time when you can come to their office and spend a few days (on your vacation or during spring break for college students) to help with solicitation calls or project work.

6. You may now put this experience on your resume. You now have more experience than before and you can use this newfound knowledge to pursue the job you've always wanted.

7. If you like this type of work and you're successful, strategize with the company to see if you can assist on a project basis (perhaps on lunch breaks or during vacation).

MPD: Volunteer your free time to obtain needed experience.

96% Of Trust, 100% To Goal

I recently interviewed a candidate and the conversation naturally included questions about revenue production. This person ended the year behind his goals and explained why:

His team had an opportunity to bid on a piece of business that wasn't the best fit for their hotel. It was a large event and would have prohibited colleagues from booking other groups (with sleeping rooms) during the same time. The client agreed to sign the contract by the end of the year if the hotel conceded to her demands. This salesperson – who would have made his numbers with the booking – opted to decline the business. At the final hour, a teammate booked the same space with more guest rooms and helped achieve the overall team goal.

Unfortunately, this person didn't meet his year-end revenue goal (96 percent). However, he felt confident and proud in his decision to earn <u>100 percent</u> of trust from his hotel and sales colleagues.

I once worked at a hotel that declined a group because the meeting planner was incredibly disrespectful and downright nasty to the staff. We tried to understand the customer's style and even assigned new banquet captains in an effort to adapt accordingly. Unfortunately, the situation never improved. We politely asked her to recommend a colleague to work with our staff but she disagreed. We finally asked the client to move to another location and offered assistance finding an alternate hotel. The executive team decided that everyone's happiness was more important than the money generated from this one event.

Are there situations where your overall goals may not have been achieved but your internal moral treasure box was plentiful? Put forth your efforts for the right reasons with solid judgment and the results will naturally arrive.

MPD: Let integrity drive your decisions.

A Cubicle With A View

The secret to getting more money may lie in the environment in which we work. The average American spends an average of 52 hours a week sitting at a desk.

During a business trip to Laguna Niguel, California, I met a doorman who worked at his hotel for 15 years. Upon my arrival we spoke about the outstanding weather that day (mid 60's, sunshine and no humidity). His only complaint was that the waves were only "biting at ankle height." He told me he gets to the beach about once a week just to touch his toes to the sand and dip them in the ocean. He couldn't imagine doing anything else. His job as a doorman aligned perfectly with his lifestyle and love of the outdoors.

The days spent in California were extremely busy with appointments, meetings and conference calls. However, I remembered the doorman's comment about the weather and decided that I needed to appreciate the environment around me. I opened the doors in my room to catch a glimpse of the ocean and hear the waves.

Are there things you can do to improve your work environment? Buy a plant, put up a picture, burn a scented candle, play soft music, use a fan, or get a dimmer switch. There are even light therapy lamps that help to rejuvenate sunshine-deprived individuals. Studies reveal that people who work in offices with plants and windows feel better about their jobs and the work they perform.

If you're on your feet all day get some gel shoe inserts, new soft socks or fresh cologne. A bellman who I knew 25 years ago kept a roll of quarters in his pocket that he squeezed all day to strengthen his grip when carrying luggage.

MPD: Create your own paradise.

A Decision Maker In Sheep's Clothing

Have you identified the decision maker when you're negotiating? Do you know who makes the hiring decision to select a new employee? Responsibilities within organizations change daily and others may be asked to get involved in the process. Is the person asking for the details the same person who's going to sign the contract or hire the new employee?

Most people enjoy the attention they get from sales people who are "wooing" them. Who wouldn't want to feel special and be entertained especially when the salesperson thinks they're the decision maker? Why should the customer ruin the illusion and inform the vendor of his true responsibilities?

I've seen leads come from five different individuals who say have the right to collect bids on behalf of their organizations. So who is the decision maker?

Have you asked the right questions?

- Who will be signing the contract? Does this person have financial responsibility? Who makes the final hiring decision? Will I have a chance to meet with him or her?
- Is there a board or a group responsible for making the decision? Would we have a chance to present to them?
- Does anyone else have the authority to make changes or alter the contract or decision?

Answer these simple questions and you'll be able to avoid needlessly exerting your time and effort. Don't forget to be kind and respectful to everyone as you never know when positions and situations will change. I've heard stories of unemployed clients returning to higher positions who only gave business to those suppliers who stayed in contact with them while they were out of a job.

MPD: Ask questions.

The Sales Call - What Is Important?

I found an old training binder from 1992 that contained a presentation entitled "The Sales Call – What Is Important?"

It states:
- Always have an appointment
- Always have a defined purpose and goal for each call
- Know your product
- Present only what your client needs (and what pertains to them)
- Get a commitment and feedback on each item you present
- Listen and look for opportunities
- Follow up, follow up and follow up

Has anything changed from 1992?

MPD: Have a plan and a process for selling.

Anyone Could Be A Client

Have you been to New York City to see a Broadway show? My friend and I recently saw "Memphis" and stuck around after the show with other people waiting near the Shubert Theatre's stage door.

Curiosity got the best of us and we waited to see the show's stars. There were the regular groupies who had their programs and sharpies ready for autographs and others who just wanted to say "thank you" to the performers.

I had a brief encounter with a young cast member who was making her Broadway debut. One moment she was a celebrity signing autographs, and the next moment she blended into the crowd as a typical New Yorker making her way to the subway to get home.

We watched as performer after performer quickly met their fans and then disappeared into the city dressed in regular street clothes.

The next day I went to Penn Station to catch my train home. A woman blatantly cut in line in front of me. This raised my blood pressure but I wasn't in a hurry and said "no problem." It could've been a major customer or a prospective client just as easily as a cast member of "Wicked."

MPD: Treat everyone politely and with respect.

Selling The Dream, Servicing The Nightmare

My wife and I took a bike ride last summer along the C&O Towpath in Washington, D.C. and quickly learned the "rules of the road." Walkers hate runners and runners loathe cyclists. The cyclists hate the walkers but can tolerate the runners. All of this reminded me of the situational differences that exist among different departments in the world of business.

You may have heard the saying "the sales department sells the dream and the operations team services the nightmare."

We took this bike ride to relax and forget about work. But I suddenly found myself immersed in the stress of the prior week. My eyes began to play tricks on me. Elderly ladies walking three people wide looked like housekeepers refusing to remove furniture from a guestroom. Two Lance Armstrong groupies looked like overanxious sales people racing to get a contract signed without researching booking patterns or the client's needs. Joggers who listened to music on their headphones resembled unfocused front office managers at a pre-con meeting who arrived late without apologizing to the meeting planners.

My wife sensed my tension and used a magnificent $3 investment called a bike bell. She <u>COMMUNICATED</u>, rang the bell and said, "passing on your left." Guess what happened? Fewer people were upset. They waived, acknowledged the bell and said "thank you" when we needed to pass. Everyone was still busy running and biking, but the entire scene was so much more civilized.

Do we tell the housekeeping department the total amount of revenue an upcoming group will generate for the hotel? Do we talk about how many employees will get to work the week that the group arrives if we are flexible enough to accommodate their needs? Do we coach salespeople on the importance of obtaining accurate historical information to forecast proper staffing levels? Does the front desk understand the importance of timeliness from a meeting planner's perspective?

MPD: Communicate the importance of customers to others.

Are You In The Basement?

Are you in the basement? Is your office below ground? Are your executive offices located next to the garage? I've never fully understood this facet of the service industry. We employ solid sales people to sell lavish ballrooms, spa services and suites, but confine them to the dark depths of a building. Are we sometimes so embarrassed that we don't dare allow visitors to see our office space? Perhaps it doesn't bother some people as much as it bothers me.

People who work from home may find enjoyment and stimulation by occasionally changing their work environments. I often see professionals "plugging in" at libraries and coffee shops around the country.

Those in search of sunlight are forced out of the office to make more sales calls and meet with the customer. My wife – who was also in hotel sales – would always say her best day was one that included a "breakfast, lunch and a tea appointment." She loved the client interaction and the relationship building. The opportunity to savor culinary samples from the restaurant was simply one of the perks of the job.

I understand and respect the fact that revenue space is at a premium for hotels and restaurants. That may be why I now see more regional offices located off property. Usually these spaces have sufficient room, lighting and furnishings that are generally suitable for clients to visit. When employees move off property they typically escape certain responsibilities such as "lobby duty" or "plate up assistance" in the kitchen.

Does having sales offices off property encourage more solicitation time? Does it permit the operations team to focus on operations and the sales team to focus on selling? Does this separation create distance in the relationship between sales and operations? My current sales team works entirely from home, enjoys the flexibility and produces tremendous results.

MPD: Change your environment.

Be Where You Are

I enjoy watching professional football. My favorite team is the Pittsburgh Steelers but I occasionally root for the Washington Redskins. During a game one Sunday between the Steelers and Dolphins, I couldn't help but notice a cameraman in the end zone who kept focusing on an attractive female fan. She wasn't watching the game; she was sending text messages on her phone. Keep in mind the average NFL game ticket is about $113.

B Where U R

I have a friend who complains that he works too much and wants to spend more time with his family. When we joined his family for dinner recently, he spent most of the evening ignoring us and responding to work messages on his phone.

B Where U R

One Saturday night our family made a concerted effort to avoid technology and electronics. Our kids invited their friends over and we played softball and football in our cul-de-sac. At sunset we used our fire pit to roast hot dogs and marshmallows for a dozen kids on our driveway.

B Where U R

Relish in the journey and live in the moment. When you ask someone "how are you?" wait for the answer and actually listen to the response. A friend recently incorporated this thinking into his message of "Be Great Today" to his employees. He wanted them to focus on finding success in their current positions and avoid thinking about their next job until given the right opportunity.

MPD: Enjoy being in the present.

Beat Over The Head With A Contract

I once heard a sales leader say, "I would never beat a salesperson over the head with a contract." This was his way of supporting the efforts of his team. He believed in empowerment and allowed his colleagues to book business on their own terms and with little supervision. He provided guidelines for them, educated them and allowed them to do what they do best: close business.

In today's competitive world employees who can make smart, quick decisions will produce winning results. Seeking certainty before taking action can negatively impact productivity.

Remember when you were buying a new car and the salesperson had to dismiss himself every five minutes to "get approval" from his manager?

Support your team members when they make quick decisions that satisfy customers or influence your organization. You should reward their efforts regardless of the outcome. Make sure you celebrate first and discuss later. New employees sometimes have an easier time asking for forgiveness rather than permission.

MPD: Support your team members.

Who Is Your Back-Up?

Everyone deserves a vacation now and then including salespeople. Who's going to handle your accounts and help you meet your revenue goals when you're basking in the sun sipping a pina colada?

Microsoft Office provides an "out of office" assistant but won't satisfy your clients when they need your help immediately. Your client may learn you're on vacation after sending an e-mail but that only means he or she must do more work. The client may have to resend the e-mail to a new recipient listed in your "out of office" message or call someone instead.

If your back-up plan involves recruiting another sales manager, keep in mind this colleague may be more consumed with obtaining his or her own goals than helping you.

Some suggestions:
- Consider partnering with a colleague who has similar experiences and who may have worked with your market in the past.
- Be a partner for them when they're on vacation first. Set the standard to follow when you're out of the office.
- Ask your colleague to proactively monitor your inbox during the day and respond directly to those customers who require immediate help. Don't wait for clients to call your office.

MPD: Make proper coverage arrangements.

Before You Turn Down Business, Read This...

Customers who try to book a September meeting in Washington, D.C. with a Monday or Tuesday arrival pattern are most likely to hear the word "no" muttered from their sales contact. Fall is one of the busiest travel periods in the nation's capital.

A GOOD salesperson will ask if you're flexible with your dates. GREAT salespeople will explain why they're asking.

A hotel needs to maximize revenue on a daily basis with a perishable inventory. The wrong selling strategy for one night can disrupt an entire week of profit. It's the job of the revenue management and sales teams to work together to determine the proper placement of rooms and space. You may have heard "it's not what you book, it's what you move" as a statement referring to this practice.

We must tell meeting planners the reasons why we're asking about their flexibility. And we must explain how they can benefit by being flexible (better rates, more meeting space, etc.).

The same strategy applies to other industries and situations. If you're selling cars for a living, find out what features are most important to the customer. The client may be willing to purchase a white car with a V8 engine that's on your lot *today* instead of waiting for his or her preferred color. If you're interviewing for a job, find out what qualities are most important to the hiring manager.

Next time you book your vacation take note of the number of websites that will ask in advance if you're flexible. This allows companies to promote specials that may fit your needs.

The same applies to job offers. Before you turn down an offer make sure you ask about the company's flexibility. You may not be willing to move to St. Louis but you can spend one week a month working there. What do you require to make the partnership with a new company work harmoniously?

MPD: Inquire about flexibility.

Passing A Skunk In A Convertible

How can the title of this page relate to your career?

For many years, I've offered career advice and suggestions for selling and leading sales organizations. I've shared best practices that I've learned over the past 25 years in the industry, but I never mentioned one factor that's beyond our control: <u>LUCK.</u>

You can take the approach with karma and believe that "good things will happen to good people." However, a bit of luck often needs to factor into the equation.

If we share ideas with others chances are luck will come our way. Luck is taking an inquiry call to fill a hole created by a recent cancellation. Luck is getting an unexpected signed contract back on the last day of the quarter to help someone reach a sales goal. Luck is being offered a job in the city you prefer. Luck is making one last solicitation call at the end of a busy day to uncover a great lead. Luck is being stuck in stop-and-go traffic for 40 minutes and then hitting the open road with just enough time to zoom past a dead skunk in your convertible.

MPD: Put forth the right efforts to doing the right things.

BTW, "Good Morning"

"Contact my client right away, send ten brochures, revise the contract and make sure our luncheon is confirmed for noon today. Thx!"

How many times have you sent your first e-mail on Monday without taking the time to be polite and considerate? Notice that this message doesn't offer a "good morning." It doesn't inquire about the person's weekend and it abruptly concludes with an abbreviated "thanks." I read an article years ago that said one of the greatest questions a leader can ask his team members on Monday morning to motivate them is: "How was your weekend?" This sincere gesture in today's hectic world is what sets great leaders apart from others.

I still find myself on busy days writing very direct, impersonal messages only to hit the delete key to correct my mistakes.

By the way, did I ask you how your day is going today?

MPD: Ask about others and listen to their responses.

Are You A Buffalo Or A Goose?

A book entitled "Flight of the Buffalo" (Belasco & Stayer, 1993) described two different types of leadership styles. One type is akin to the style embraced by wild buffaloes. There is one head buffalo that is responsible for dictating every move the herd makes. Buffaloes are very loyal animals that have a tendency to follow their leaders into precarious situations (over cliffs) without regard for their own well-being. American Indians used to hunt buffalo by killing the leader. The rest of the herd quickly became confused and turned into easy prey for the hunters.

Do you know any managers who are "buffalo leaders?"

The other type of leader embraces a group approach. Geese fly in a "V" formation but leadership is always ahead of the group's needs. For example, one goose might be very good at locating food and another might be an expert at navigation. Therefore, each goose participates based on the needs of the entire group. When geese fly their wings provide uplift to help others coast along. The entire flock can fly 71 percent farther than a bird flying solo.

What is the best way for you to lead?

Are you a buffalo or a goose?

MPD: Lead by example.

Carrot Or Stick Leadership

If you've ever been active in youth sports – as an athlete or as a parent – you will understand this message. I played both basketball and volleyball in high school. My dream at a young age was to play basketball for the Boston Celtics. But when my growth climaxed at 6'2" I realized this goal had to change. My basketball coach was a maniac on and off the court. He could never relax, he was always yelling and he insisted on making the team run "suicides" until someone threw up at the end of every practice. He made everyone feel inferior even *after* we won games. And he instilled fear in his players through plenty of verbal abuse.

My volleyball coach was a mild-mannered gentleman who loved teaching the sport. We had fun and learned in a positive environment. I can't remember a single time he lost his cool. We never ran "suicides" because he created enough volleyball drills to strengthen our conditioning. If we lost (which didn't happen often) we felt bad for ourselves and thought we were letting our coach down. It came as no surprise that Coach Mike Larko was inducted into the Plum High School Sports Hall of Fame and the Pennsylvania Volleyball Coaches Hall of Fame.

I made a conscious decision to avoid basketball and pursue volleyball. The sport provided me with great experiences and friends. In 1985, I was listed by Volleyball Monthly as one of the top 50 high school volleyball players in the country. During my sophomore year I earned a walk-on spot for Penn State's Division I team. We placed third in the 1987 NCAA Championship.

How far will your team go if you create a "carrot" enticing leadership environment?

MPD: Share positivity and encouragement.

Ceiling Spice And Pittsburgh Pizza

An area in Pittsburgh called the "Strip District" is comprised of wholesalers, fresh produce stands and souvenir tables. It truly represents the multicultural diversity within Pittsburgh. Even though this city is known for its sports teams (Steelers, Penguins and Pirates), there are a tremendous number of food venues that rival many culinary experiences worldwide. So what makes this section of downtown Pittsburgh so special? The PEOPLE!

What makes your business or hotel special? Is it the chandelier, the high thread count sheets or the flat-screen televisions? The last time I checked most competitors had these items.

It's the uniqueness, passion and enthusiasm exhibited by your staff that makes all the difference.

Bella Notte Pizza in the Strip District is very special. Everyone notices the "ceiling spice" (when the dough is tossed high enough to hit the tented ceiling and pick up some additional flavor). But you can also tell that the staff truly wants to make the best pizza in town.

A typical restaurant wouldn't encourage these preparation techniques.

But this business encourages its employees to be creative.

Are you seizing upon the uniqueness of your staff to allow them to make a difference? Are you showing your personality and creativity at work?

MPD: Explore the uniqueness of your staff.

A Cheeseburger Without Cheese

A sales colleague came to me once to offer a little comic relief. She was working with an experienced meeting planner who insisted on referring to "theater style" seating (chairs lined up facing the same direction) as "classroom style without the tables." "Classroom style" typically mimics a school classroom with chairs and tables. My colleague didn't correct the client and booked the business.

There's no need to correct customers or to explain policies and procedures. Clients don't want to know reasons why something can't be done. Often these reasons come across as excuses. Spend more time finding ways to <u>make things happen</u> and less time explaining why certain things can't happen.

Remember it's not how *we* want to do business (on our terms and our definitions) but how our customers want to do business. We need to accept obscure terms or descriptions as long as we can deliver what the customer needs and ultimately close the sale.

The next time you're at a restaurant order a cheeseburger without the cheese to see if the server corrects you. The most talented service professionals will deliver exactly what you order without hesitation.

MPD: Conduct business as your customers want to do business.

The Truth About Soliciting Business

- 80% of all sales are made after the fifth call

- 48% of all salespeople make one call and quit

- 25% of all salespeople call twice and quit

- 17% of all salespeople call three times and quit

- 10% of all salespeople keep calling

- 80% of all sales are made by 10% of all salespeople!

MPD: Never stop calling.

Crossing The Street While Listening For Electric Cars

Technology has changed our lives. Some perceive these changes as positive and others view them as negative. When my son was 12 years old I wanted to see if he looked both ways before crossing the street. He didn't so I questioned him. He said he never looks because he can always hear cars approaching. But what about electric cars? He conceded that electric cars are quieter than regular cars and finally agreed to change his routine. I didn't have to worry about electric cars as a kid.

Technology is also changing the way we do business. Some customers conduct themselves without even speaking to salespeople. New lead distribution systems allow consolidated, expedited communication. Sometimes these systems deliver warning messages such as "do not contact client." Have you ever tried to contact a company only to be caught in voicemail purgatory when none of the buttons will take you to a live person?

The way Generation Y communicates has changed as well. Many young people now have cellular phones but may never use them for actual phone calls.

How can we as salespeople develop and foster relationships without talking to customers? What are you doing as professionals to combat the forced sterilization of sales? What are you doing as a young professional to effectively communicate verbally with others?

MPD: Take advantage of technology
while not allowing it to replace
face-to-face relationships.

Crossing Your "I"s And Dotting Your "T"s

Attention to detail will help you win new customers and keep existing ones. Was there anything incorrect in the title of this page? Were you in such a hurry to finish the project (reading) that you didn't even notice the mistake? Customers these days will notice the smallest mistakes. Employers also notice small errors and will not show forgiveness.

I received inspiration from a restaurant employee who graciously excused herself when she cut in front of me in a salad bar line to remove a piece of wilted lettuce. I still visit that restaurant because of the care and concern exhibited by this employee. Her attention to detail was impressive even for a relatively simple quality issue.

"Excellence is in the details. Give attention to the details and excellence will come." - Perry Paxton

Do you ensure that your form contracts contain the correct details? Is the cover letter addressed to Ms. Renee Taylor but the introduction reads "Dear Ms. Wolff?"

Have you ever been to a restaurant and the server asked about your food allergies but delivered the entrée with the one ingredient you couldn't eat?

Pull out those wilted pieces of lettuce before your customers stop eating at your salad bar and double check every document before it's sent!

MPD: Pay attention to the details.

Empowerment

If you're like me chances are you're too busy to always accomplish the tasks on your "to do" list. Leaders may not have enough time to review each and every situation with their team members. That's why managers need to be empowered to make their own decisions.

Of course, I'm assuming you have the right people in the right jobs. An old general manager of mine told his sales team that - if for any reason he was unavailable - he would empower them to make their own decisions to book business. If he disagreed he would simply share his opinion and never override the team's choice.

Are you allowed to make business decisions quickly? Or do you need the approval of others, which may delay the response time to the customer?

A few suggestions to allow for quicker responses via empowerment:
1. Set clear expectations for the goal and offer proper training
2. Provide the parameters and the tools necessary to accomplish the tasks
3. Discuss any exceptions after the outcome while still showing support

This is a valuable lesson for everyone. Empower your team to make the right decisions to please and satisfy the customer. Your happy clients will then share their positive experiences with others.

MPD: Make decisions confidently and independently.

Delivering The Unexpected

Send a gift when it's not someone's birthday. <u>Do the unexpected.</u>

The standards for "expected" have decreased to the point where simply doing the expected is a bonus. I suggest <u>doing the unexpected.</u>

Customers may expect a holiday card and a gift in December to show appreciation for their business. Send them a gesture of appreciation in January after all the other gifts have arrived. Usually an office can only eat so much cheese and caramel popcorn in a month.

My sister was diagnosed with colon cancer in 2011. My wife bought her an early Valentine's Day card and enclosed a pair of pink, fuzzy socks she could wear during her treatments. It was unexpected and even prompted a "thank you" phone call from a relative who doesn't phone often.

Our team holds a wine tasting event every January to celebrate the New Year. This year 13 out of 14 invitees attended because our gathering didn't conflict with other holiday parties held in December.

When was the last time you sent a "just because" gift card to a friend? When someone comes to mind take the time to mail a note, send an e-mail or make a quick phone call. The last time I was in Chicago I thought of my college buddy who was kind enough to show me around the city when I moved there. I called him to say hello and to tell him I appreciated his friendship.

My daughter's softball coach is very committed to teaching skills and positive sportsmanship to his players including his own daughter who's on the team. One of the parents noticed that the coach never has the time to take photos of his own child because he's always preoccupied with coaching. Another parent also noticed and decided to take some action shots of the coach's daughter that he framed at the end of the year as a thank you gift. The coach may not remember how many games the team won or lost that season but he'll always remember the thoughtfulness of that gift.

MPD: Express thoughtfulness when not expected.

Bart Berkey

Have You Thanked Anyone Today?

As a coach for my son's middle school volleyball team, I studied the players and tried to find out what motivated them. It didn't take long to separate the outstanding athletes from the adequate ones. One day I brought my video camera to practice and decided to film a portion of a drill. When I watched the tape at home I saw something hiding in plain sight. The players were rooting for each other. My son was thrilled to be playing with kids who gave each other "high fives" throughout practice and during the games.

A few days later I received an e-mail from one of my sales managers. It was a copy of a note he sent to a person's boss complimenting the employee on her hard work securing a great piece of business. This inspired a group of us to send more notes complimenting her on her efforts. The effort behind nine simple keystrokes (THANK YOU) can truly make someone's day!

If no one has done anything nice for you today, allow me to be the first. "THANK YOU" for what you do everyday. Thank you for representing your product sincerely to your clients. Thank you for being a sincere friend and caring family member. Thank you for studying and making a difference in your industry. Thank you for treating your colleagues with respect. And thank you for continuing to learn by reading this book.

MPD: Encourage others with appreciation.

Hospitality On A Hog

My 80-year-old father and I love to ride our motorcycles on the back roads of suburban Pittsburgh. My kids recently followed behind in my mother's car to see what it's like.

When we finished my kids said they saw me "waving" to other bikers on the road. I actually never thought about this until my children questioned me about it. They said, "When we drive our SUV, we don't waive to other SUV's on the road, so why do motorcyclists do this?"

I did some research and found an article by Tom Ruttan entitled "The Wave." He describes it as "a demonstration of comradeship and a mutual understanding of what it is to enjoy riding a motorcycle. All bikers have to struggle with the same things like cold, rain, heat, car drivers who do not see them, but riding always remains an almost pure pleasure."

We as service professionals have a mutual understanding of the joy in serving others. We all struggle with the same issues like long hours, low pay, continuous challenges and unappreciative guests. But we never forget that serving others remains an absolute pleasure.

Take care of other professionals in your industry. Upgrade a colleague, leave a generous tip or offer an enthusiastic "thank you" when you receive great service. Take the time to be kind to others in any profession. Encourage each other and show respect since you've all experienced similar challenges.

MPD: Show kindness to others in your field of work.

How To Lose 10 Pounds

The South Beach Diet is a program that limits fruits, sugars and carbohydrates. The first two weeks are extremely rigid to help rid your body of excess sugars and alleviate cravings for these foods.

I followed the diet for two weeks and easily lost ten pounds.

On week three our family went to the beach for vacation. I didn't worry about having a few slices of pizza or a few handfuls of boardwalk fries. Our hotel didn't have a scale so I couldn't weigh myself. When we got home I decided to avoid the scale until I started eating salads and fresh vegetables again. Turns out I weighed exactly the same. I had conquered the diet and still had fun eating some treats.

A month later I thought I could cheat again. It started when someone brought donuts into the office. The next day we had brownies for an afternoon treat. This continued for several weeks until I finally gave up weighing myself and maintaining a healthy eating regimen. If I could maintain my weight after vacation it should be easy to do at home, right?

I was wrong, and I was heavier.

This valuable lesson taught me to always think about what I eat. Of course, we can treat ourselves on special occasions, but we need to remember the basics of healthy eating every day.

Now for the correlation to our professional lives. I've seen many successful salespeople work hard to secure a top account. They do the research, entertain board members, anticipate their needs and work diligently until they receive the signed contract. They work for the first two weeks (as I did during my diet) and then they go on "vacation." They don't say "thank you" once the contract arrives. And they're nowhere to be found when the function arrives at the hotel.

The same approach applies to personal relationships. Maintain the intensity with your friends and the special people in your life.

MPD: Maintain the relationship process consistently.

Just Get It Right

How would you handle this situation?

My family and I had dinner at one of our favorite restaurants. We arrived on a Friday evening without reservations and were quickly seated. Our server arrived with a negative attitude and obviously had no interest in providing good service.

My wife ordered the blackberry lemonade martini. She thought it tasted strange. She asked for another and it still wasn't right. She told our server it was one of her favorite drinks because she couldn't find blackberry vodka in stores anymore. He said it now contained raspberry vodka. The restaurant should've changed the name to reflect the new vodka.

The fish wasn't cooked properly. The bread was stale. The salads were delivered incorrectly three times. And the server still didn't seem to care.

A manager always steps in at this restaurant when there's a problem or a complaint. Management did the right thing this time around by apologizing and removing our entrees from the bill. The server was obviously annoyed with our "demands" and reluctantly stopped by the table to deliver the check. He also charged us for my son's juice, which was refilled twice for a total of $6.50.

What would you have done as the manager? What would you have done as the server?

MPD: Correct challenges in the proper manner.

Leadership, Sometimes Less Is More

My sales team used to participate in our company's summer softball league. We had as many as 30 people who would come out to play and support the group. I huddled with the players at the beginning of each season and we identified what we hoped to achieve through our participation.

1. Have fun
2. Bond and network with colleagues
3. Enjoy exercise and activity

We knew everyone would need to play in order to accomplish these objectives. We also understood that we were all competitive salespeople. But we were willing to lose as long as we didn't deviate from our goals. As the coach and captain, I focused on developing the lineup, keeping score, making substitutions, and ensuring that everyone was participating and having fun.

The team didn't know that I never played organized baseball or softball. And I quickly realized that other players on our team had more experience and superior softball skills. So I relinquished my leadership role during the second game and asked others to contribute. One person coordinated the lineup, another kept score, someone brought the equipment and another organized the fans. When I relinquished my duties the most amazing thing happened. Everyone played and we won!

Are you a leader who can be successful by stepping back? Can you contribute more by volunteering and literally stepping up to the plate?

MPD: Find leadership qualities in others.

Humpty Dumpty Was Pushed

Time to get real and destroy any preconceived notions that Humpty Dumpty actually fell. Let's be serious — he was definitely pushed.

We may fluff pillows and serve guests; however, the harsh reality is that the hospitality business is a business. Take a drink from a "big boy" mug; no more "sippie cups" allowed.

"A group canceled and I can't make my monthly goals."

"The economy faltered and my client didn't get approval to book his meeting."

"My customer's budget was reduced so her food and beverage spend is less than anticipated."

"The competition is offering lower rates."

"I didn't get the job because they wanted someone with different experience."

"I was fired because my boss was jealous of me."

Waaaa, waaaa, waaaaa…

What are you going to do about it?

The harsh reality is that we need to find creative ways to overcome obstacles. This is our job. It's our responsibility to provide revenue and profit to our ownership groups, our management companies and the employees of our properties.

Do members of your sales team make another cold call when they're tired? Do members of your leadership team and general manager come out to meet customers when they're on property? Or are they stuck behind closed doors in an internal meeting discussing how to find more business? I wonder what Alice in Wonderland's deep dark secret is?

MPD: Accept responsibility for your own future.

Leash Your Puppies To Your Leader

One Sunday morning I was doing some yard work and wanted our two dogs (at the time) to get some fresh air and play outside. Bruno was our extremely obedient 11-year-old purebred Staffordshire Bull Terrier. Lulu was a rescued two-year-old Chihuahua, terrier, dachshund, puddle-drinking and bug-chasing mix.

We don't know anything about Lulu's background. When we adopted her she didn't know how to walk on a leash or climb stairs. She was far from being housebroken and created a mess around the house. On the other hand, Bruno came from an award-winning pedigree and passed two obedience classes with flying colors. He was our prince and behaved perfectly.

Bruno taught Lulu how to wait for food, how to go down the stairs, how to use the lawn (and not carpeting) for bathroom breaks and how to play properly. In many ways Bruno was our anchor, and I tied Lulu to him so she wouldn't run away. This made me think about mentoring and the benefit of partnering a junior person with a senior leader. A rookie salesperson might not know how to dress, how to act, how to solicit, how to interact with operations, etc.

Do you assign a "buddy" or a "mentor" to your freshmen employees so they can quickly learn the ropes and produce revenue?

MPD: Connect your new employees to senior staff.

Making It Easier

My gas tank was running on empty one cold December morning so I pulled in to fill up at my local service station. I forgot my gloves and my hands were especially cold. When I pulled up to the pump I overheard the weatherman on a nearby TV telling me the high for the day would be 25 degrees.

I inserted my credit card into the pump without any problems. It took a few moments to register and the computer asked if it was a credit or debit card. I patiently responded.

The next prompt asked me to swipe a frequent gas card. I declined and waited another five seconds for the screen to clear.

Then the computer wanted to know about my interest in a carwash (which was closed since it was below freezing). I hit the "no" button and began to lose my patience.

Finally, after 30 seconds of screen prompts, I could finally pump my gas.

Would you continue pumping gas here?

Do you make it easy for others to do business with you? Do you ask them hundreds of questions in the wrong order only to discover after 20 minutes that you can't provide the best solution?

Do your customers a favor and organize thoughtful questions in a manner that qualifies the business quickly and efficiently. Saving time will truly benefit everyone!

Do you make it easy for others to be friends with you or to be in a relationship with you? Are you always complaining? Be mindful of how you're acting and make it easy and enjoyable for others to be with you!

MPD: Simplify the process.

Getting People To Like You In 30 Seconds

Have you ever heard the expression you have only "30 seconds to make a first impression?" The attention span for the average person is even shorter than this. Most people will only pay attention if what you're saying is interesting and beneficial.

I decided to experiment with a "theory" of mine in an artificially created situation. A new employee just started and most of my team didn't have the chance to meet her. I introduced her at a morning meeting as a new client who owned a meeting planning business.

I asked the team to introduce themselves and ask questions. One person asked about the hotels she booked in the past. Another asked about her clients. One colleague asked why she entered the industry and how she started her own company. So I asked our "pretend client" to identify the one salesperson that stood out from the crowd. The most memorable colleague was the one who tried to get to know her as a person before a client.

Be sincere and interesting in your approach, and remember you now have only 26 more seconds to make an impact.

MPD: Take a genuine interest in others.

The Value Of Voice (Over Thumbs)

We can all agree that things move quickly. People are working constantly. A commercial flight used to provide a reprieve from work. Now, the Internet is everywhere, even at 30,000 feet.

I received a troubling e-mail from a colleague a few weeks ago and my first reaction was to fire off a very terse message. I wrote the e-mail and then waited to hit the send button. I needed time to assess the likelihood that this message would produce my desired result. I initially drafted the message as an emotional reaction to my colleague's message but decided it would be best to pick up the phone.

I immediately reached my team member and sought to understand the meaning behind his message. We discussed the situation thoroughly and made significant headway during this two-way interaction. His initial message to me was not intended to be unhelpful and I incorrectly interpreted his words.

It's evident many people prefer to do business via e-mail. However, this shouldn't prevent us from building meaningful relationships via phone and in person. Even the younger generation today may not understand the benefits of voice-to-voice interaction during this era of evolving technology.

May the business be awarded to the salesperson who seeks to understand the client's needs rather than the salesperson who writes the best e-mails.

MPD: Rely on the phone over e-mail
and text to build relationships.

Morning Meetings And Breakfast Sandwiches

What do you need in the morning to get started?

I was invited to an early morning meeting recently and greeted by a fresh plate of warm breakfast sandwiches. Most people would be surprised to see such a simple gesture delight a group of luxury hoteliers. A very hospitable team member knew the group would be discussing some serious business topics and thought everyone would enjoy this unexpected treat.

What does the team need today? What do you need today?

Is it time to offer gracious appreciation or a day to strategize? Be aware of what your team members need and deliver it. Be aware of what you need and ask for it. The gesture doesn't need to be expensive but it should be thoughtful. These sandwiches cost less than $30.

We would often recruit team members at one of my former hotels to help park cars during large banquet events. A miraculous thing happened at these events that no one ever saw. Guests would never wait for more than a minute to drop off their cars.

Our system worked flawlessly. Once the first valet parker entered the parking garage, a chain of helpers (engineers, sales managers, kitchen staff and other volunteers) would guide the car to its final parking spot. This enabled the "official" valet parker to return quickly and greet the next arriving car. The customers only saw five people greeting them with sincere smiles. But behind the scenes 53 people in tennis shoes and jeans worked like machines to park the cars safely and efficiently. The employees enjoyed helping as much as they appreciated the free pizza provided by the general manager to show his appreciation at the end of every event.

See how a dozen donuts can affect your results the next time you have a meeting before dawn.

MPD: Direct your efforts outward.

The #1 Rule For Success In Sales

I interviewed a gentleman once who shared his philosophy for success in sales. His answer was simple and direct: "respect the lead."

This made perfect sense to me. Each lead comes from a potential customer and should be given adequate attention and effort regardless of the outcome. Each lead comes from someone who has a specific need and who has the time to communicate with you. Of course, some leads may not be the perfect fit. But when you "respect the lead" you take the time to fully understand the customer's needs. Ask questions and suggest "give and take" tactics. This way most leads can and will turn into actual revenue.

This gentleman's approach made the client feel special and appreciated. He exhausted <u>all aspects of each lead</u> and built a relationship that could facilitate future business.

MPD: Treat each lead as an
opportunity to earn business.

Most Common Mistake Before Applying For A Job

I'm one of the few individuals who has a very unique name. There's only one Bart Berkey listed on the Internet. Prospective clients can type my name into Google and learn about my entrepreneurial life coaching business, read about my past jobs, view my friends and even see my contributions to the industry. One summer my family and I went to the MIT Museum in Cambridge, Massachusetts. An interactive exhibit prompted you to type in your name to view your digital footprint. My son appeared but we also discovered an author, a marine biologist and a scientist with the same name.

According to an article on mashable.com, "45% of companies now screen social media profiles" as part of their "online due diligence for prospective candidates." In this fiercely competitive environment have you typed your name into Google to see what appears? Have you updated your LinkedIn profile and removed from Facebook any inappropriate photos from your crazy college days?

MPD: Review your digital presence.

How To Act In Business And Tradeshow Etiquette

Have you ever noticed exhibitors acting unprofessionally at trade shows?

A few reminders or suggestions:
- Don't eat or drink at the booth and reserve gum for the baseball field
- Don't read the newspaper or text when the volume of traffic slows
- Don't interrupt other exhibitors when they're taking to customers. Be especially considerate when you're trying to obtain or trade promotional items. You can get that logo hat and barter when the show concludes.

Some additional ideas that can help you stand out from the inconsiderate exhibitors:

- <u>Look everyone in the eye</u> during your conversations. Ask if you can look at the person's name badge to help you remember his or her name. Too many sales people will only talk to someone if he or she has the right badge. Spend your time wisely but treat everyone with respect.
- <u>Consider the "two pocket" technique</u> for organizing business cards during the event. Put the "hot prospects" in a pocket close to your heart (shirt or jacket) because you "love" those customers who represent the greatest potential. Place the "cold prospects" in your back pocket for later (to sit on).
- <u>Be thoughtful</u> when deciding what type of information to distribute at tradeshows. Is it easy for the attendees to carry? Should you offer to mail or e-mail the items as a follow up? Should you simply direct customers to your website so they can peruse the information at their leisure?
- <u>Does your promotional item tie into your theme</u> or destination? Martini glasses look fun but are they relevant? I found success with dpriceisright.com.

MPD: Represent yourself and your company proudly.

Practice Makes Perfect

How often can salespeople actually practice their selling skills?

My son plays volleyball and each week they work on new skills like passing, setting and spiking. Each weekend his team has a league match and the parent coaches furiously observe what's good and what's bad. On one occasion the coaches noticed the kids weren't "calling" for the ball (indicating they would handle the pass) when the other team was serving. They worked on calling the ball the following week ("mine") to ensure flawless communication.

If you're looking for a new job consider the last time you rehearsed for an interview. Can you role-play with a friend and answer standard interview questions? Use the Internet to find sample interview questions and practice your answers until they become perfect.

"Practice does not make perfect. Only perfect practice makes perfect."
- Vince Lombardi

We as sales professionals are on the court everyday. Most people - after a brief orientation and training program - are immediately placed into competition and asked to score points. How often are we given the chance to refine our skills and practice?

There are many tricks hotels can use to evaluate a team's selling skills. Consider videotaping a few role-playing scenarios and watch the tape just like a professional sports team. Can you set up a time to role-play and practice the art of selling? The most senior team members can provide feedback like a coach so even their performance improves the next time they step onto the selling court!

MPD: Practice your skills to improve your craft.

The Phones Aren't Ringing

A prospective sales candidate casually said, "The phones aren't ringing." This isn't the best message to send when you're trying to make a positive impression during an interview.

"The phones aren't ringing?"

What are you going to do about it? Will you complain to your colleagues and submit to defeat? Will you do something about it? Leaders are made and sales managers created during times like these.

Take the time now to make the phones ring on the other end. Organize a blitz to target new businesses. Brew a strong cup of coffee, put on your headset, close your office door and get to work.

"No companies are calling me in for an interview after I submitted my resume?"

"The person I'm interested in dating never replied to my text message?"

"Do not fear the winds of adversity. Remember, a kite rises against the wind rather than with it." - Author Unknown

MPD: Create your own future.

You Have A Purple Hippo Request

I would use many resources in my recruiting days to locate the best talent in the industry. The Internet provides many useful tools to identify passive and active candidates. Websites like LinkedIn can be very useful especially when you need to search by experience and geographic preferences.

I still receive annoying and inappropriate e-mail requests from former candidates that read "Jack invited you to donate money so he can buy a cow for his virtual farm." I created the Purple Hippo Request (in this section's title) to help us examine the power of social media.

It amazes me that so many people are continuously using these sites instead of doing their jobs. Active job seekers should know that recruiters might research your "Internet presence." According to ExecuNet.com, 83 percent of recruiters use search engines to learn more about candidates and 43 percent of candidates are disqualified based on the results.

Would you hire someone who consistently types BOOMS (Bored Out Of My Skull) as his status update?

Google your name and remove any questionable photos or remarks that may dissuade a potential employer from hiring you. Continue to refuse those Internet requests during work hours and hopefully your friends will begin to get the message that perhaps they should be working too.

MPD: Make a great first impression online.

Qualify, Then Qualify Again

A sales manager lost a piece of business. He did everything right by asking the customer pertinent questions about the company's needs, the needs of the attendees, the company's buying concerns, competition, and even the timeline for the decision making process.

Several weeks later the customer hired an intermediary (third party) to help with the arrangements. The sales manager assumed all of the items they discussed during the initial conversation were still important. He was baffled when he learned his hotel didn't get the business.

Turns out the company wanted a hotel close to its Washington, D.C. headquarters.

The sales manager retraced his steps, reviewed his notes and concluded that he gave the customer all the right information. He provided a hotel that was within the company's budget; he accommodated their special menu requests; he offered additional concessions that were important to them; and he suggested a property convenient to the airport. Not once did the requirement of "being close to their headquarters" enter into their discussions. It was the third-party planner who prompted the company to re-examine its needs, and the sales manager who forgot to follow up and ask if anything changed.

Qualify and then qualify again.

MPD: Examine needs throughout the entire process.

Drive Your Own Day; Proactive Versus Reactive

Do you have a game plan before you login to your computer or do you allow e-mails to monopolize your time?

Do you wait for the phone to ring to find business or do you target accounts that are suitable for your company and reach out to them? Do you feel that your day is productive if you respond to every e-mail message? Note that "respond" is the key term here and describes a reactive approach.

Who is driving your day?

Most successful people approach each new morning with a "to do" list not only for the day but often for the entire month. Most successful coaches come to the gym or field with a game plan.

Each of us starts with 24 hours in a day. It's up to us to decide how to spend them.

Proactively cross items off as "done" and feel good about completing those tasks YOU identified to be important. Your ability to clear out your e-mail "inbox" does not constitute success.

MPD: Control the day with
your priorities.

Risk, Reward, And Microwave Popcorn

Do you get hungry in the middle of the day?

I recently had a mid-afternoon craving for popcorn and tossed a bag in the microwave for 30 seconds. The bag appeared to grow but I had a feeling some of the kernels weren't popping.

Did I want to keep the bag in the microwave and risk burning my entire snack just to eat a few extra kernels? I weighed my hunger against the risk of burning the batch and hit "stop."

A customer needed to cancel a meeting on the same month it was scheduled. We had to charge the client the full cancellation fee because the property needed the revenue. However, the salesperson who booked the group employed a different tactic and chose to allow the group to reschedule its event within the next 90 days (when the hotel also needed revenue).

Yes, the hotel ran the risk of losing revenue, but this option enabled the sales team to maintain the relationship with the client and possibly earn future business. They also hit the "stop" button and realized the "increased revenue" popcorn would not be worth the risk of ruining the entire "relationship bag!" The same applies to friendships and personal relationships.

MPD: Build long-term relationships
by considering short-term
concessions.

Ruthless Approaches

How do you feel when a solicitor calls just as you're sitting down to dinner?

Have you ever received a magazine article in the mail with a handwritten note that says, "Thought you'd enjoy this! From J"

I once received a form in the mail that asked me to name a beneficiary for my meager IRA. The document was partially complete with my name, social security number and home address. Attached were a financial advisor's business card and a handwritten note that said, "Call me!"

I later learned that this advisor's approach was to mail out these forms looking for new clients. My suggestion is to be honest and upfront with your approach.

"The purpose of my call is to introduce myself and my company. I would like to see if it makes sense to have a conversation to learn more about your needs and my potential ability to assist."

Versus:

"Hi. How are you doing today? How is the weather in your city today?"

Salespeople aren't always held in the highest regard. But a salesperson doesn't have to be someone who takes away your hard-earned money. Sales professionals can be a regarded as fair people who offer a service in return for a fair price.

MPD: Approach sales with honesty and sincerity.

Loyalty Lessons From A NYC Cab Driver

Imagine it's 90 degrees and humid in New York City. Your feet are tired after walking blocks to find the "American Girl Place" to please your daughter. You hiked even further on hot pavement to find the "Nintendo" store to make your son happy. You're finally ready to head back to the hotel and step onto the street to hail a cab. It's 5 p.m. and you're in the heart of Times Square.

A cab quickly pulls over and asks "where to?" I said, "Battery Park," which I thought would be a healthy $25 fare. He said, "no way."

My passion for service took hold and I mentioned that cab drivers can't pick and choose their fares. He retorted that I should have noticed the "off duty" light on his cab. This was his trick and I'm sure the approach many drivers use to "unofficially" refuse a fare. I told him I meant to say LaGuardia Airport. You can use your imagination to guess his reply.

Minutes later another cab driver arrived, greeted us warmly and said "no problem" when we told him our destination. He received the largest tip I've ever given to a service professional.

Are you and your staff kind to price sensitive markets (or customers) throughout the year or only when the economy declines? Drivers who accept mediocre fares during rush hour may be producing great rewards today due to loyalty. Are you the type of person who only talks to your "friends" when you need something?

MPD: Treat everyone with consistent kindness.

Sell To Me But Don't Talk To Me

Many customers now prefer to receive information electronically. This allows them to work quickly and efficiently. Some people no longer have time to establish relationships and would rather receive "rates, dates and space" via e-mail. Are we allowing customers to push us into a transactional mode of selling with our service becoming a commodity buy? Most of us got into the service industry because we prefer to interact with people.

Some RFP's now mandate that sales managers refrain from contacting the client. How can salespeople determine a prospective client's needs beyond the requirements listed on a document?

I would want to ask:
- What's important to you about this event?
- How will the success of this meeting affect your overall organization?
- Tell me about the attendees and what they may hope to achieve.
- What factors will contribute to the selection of a venue?

Without this basic information our customers are missing out on the service element of the sales process and the expertise we can offer to assist them.

Pick up the phone, sell yourself and sell your services. Approach all conversations with a sincere, deep interest in the meeting planner's success and the success of the event for the company.

I just leased a new car. During the initial phase, I wouldn't provide my phone number to dealerships and preferred to be contacted via e-mail. When I narrowed down my choices only then was I ready to speak to a person.

MPD: Establish more meaningful relationships.

Sharing Ideas

I completed a training class with a terrific group of students and returned to work feeling rejuvenated. What I enjoyed most was hearing veterans and new hires share their selling experiences with each other. Egos were "checked at the door" and everyone benefited by exchanging thoughts.

"If you and I both have apples, and we exchange them, we are both each left with a single apple. If you and I both have an idea, and we exchange them, we both leave with two ideas."

We took this messaging to the next level and discussed ways to overcome customer objections. Using the "share an idea" philosophy, the group discussed ways to work with other team members to help solve problems and provide solutions.
- Allow the chef to provide the tour of the kitchen since he or she is the expert.
- Consult the banquet team if you don't have enough space for a meeting.
- A large piece of business required additional space for a cocktail reception. A bellman overheard the salesperson's dilemma and suggested using part of the parking garage that had just been re-paved. The garage wasn't ready for cars but customers enjoying a reception wouldn't be problematic.

The same philosophy applies to other industries. Consult with your colleagues to get ideas on how to improve your organization. Talk with people who can provide input from different perspectives and conclude discussions with several "apples."

MPD: Involve others and share ideas.

Airing Clean Laundry At Work

A few years ago my family and I spent several nights at Deep Creek Lake in Maryland. The area attracts vacationers throughout the year with plenty of outdoor activities. This particular weekend occurred in late summer right after the busy season. We found much of the staff to be worn out and tired after a hectic summer. A server at a restaurant actually yawned and sat down next to us to take our order.

When we went to buy a soda for the kids we saw employees at a convenience store drinking milkshakes. My wife asked about business after Labor Day when things really slow down and the employees told her they pass the time by folding their laundry on the store's front counter.

Guests and customers shouldn't be inconvenienced because they visit at the wrong time. There should never be a "wrong time" to provide service.

Are you training your employees to provide service when a customer calls at closing time? Do your guests feel welcome when they arrive at your pool 30 minutes before you close? Should a family who arrives at a Mother's Day brunch for the last seating be denied fresh coffee and a slice of pie? If your team is tired what are you doing to re-energize them?

MPD: Perform like you're "on stage" regardless of your energy level.

Short And Sweet

"It would be my pleasure, at your earliest convenience, to learn more about the requirements for your upcoming conference so we can deliver a unique, satisfying experience for you and your attendees."

OR

"I would love the chance to learn more about your needs."

"Let thy speech be short, comprehending much in few words."

- Apocrypha

MPD: Spend more time listening.

Silence Is Golden (And Sometimes Green)

He who speaks first in a negotiation loses. This was taught to me at a very young age and I've been able to use it in many situations. Try it...

This tactic can also been applied to everyday conversations and especially those instances when you need to win a negotiation. I've heard stories of people getting pay raises by remaining silent after they make the request.

A future groom calls your hotel looking for a block of rooms for his wedding party. You enthusiastically offer a rate of $189, which is discounted from the regular rate of $209 for the weekend. Concurrently, his bride-to-be starts calling several nearby hotels and identifies the maximum amount ($150) their guests should spend on a hotel. But the groom really likes your hotel and enjoys working with you.

You know your suburban hotel could really use the weekend business. A soccer team just cancelled its entire room block for the same weekend.

Your first instinct is to quote a lower price as soon as you sense silence on the other end of the phone. Instead, you remember this lesson and wait for a reaction. Five seconds seems like an eternity. He finally agrees and you finalize the details.

Show confidence in your product. Be proud of the rates you offer. The customer doesn't need to know that weekends are slow or that a group just cancelled. You know your price is fair and your service exceeds expectations. Your client and his guests will be happy, and you'll do everything within your power to ensure this as a salesperson, as a communicator, and as an ambassador for hospitality.

Try the intentional stall or the deliberate pause and examine your success.

Silence is not only golden. It can also be green (the color of money)!

MPD: Pause during negotiations.

When Is A Solicitation Call A Solicitation Call?

I distinctly remember a valuable lesson I learned when I was just starting out in the industry. I had some free time before a holiday when business typically slows down. I decided to run some reports and study past groups that booked our hotel (actuals) versus those we "lost" to the competition.

I also decided to try soliciting new business.

My first call went straight to voicemail and I checked a box on an activities sheet to note my first solicitation call. I then wrote an e-mail to the same company. I designed a great e-mail template that encouraged clients to contact me with any hotel needs in our neighborhood. I felt great and checked another box "complete" to mark my second solicitation call. I was on a roll and completed two activities in just over two minutes!

I turned in my activity report at the end of the week and proudly announced to my boss that I made 56 solicitation calls. I bragged about my efforts and challenged my colleagues to see if anyone could do a better job that week. My boss then asked me about the number of "contacts" I made during these calls. I said I made 56 solicitation calls and felt I should be commended!

I quickly learned and was humbled to realize that it was not enough to just perform the activity without getting the results. Calling is not enough to find business. Following up may not always be enough to find business. Consistent, enthusiastic effort and follow up facilitates real contact and establishes meaningful dialogue with customers that produce business.

MPD: Keep calling until contact is made.

Spinning Signs And Site Inspections

Have you ever noticed someone trying to catch your attention by wildly throwing a sign above his head and around his body?

I saw one very talented young man on a street corner recently who was very good at the art of "spinning signs." I did some research on the idea of "human directionals" and uncovered some interesting information. Apparently "motion attracts attention," which is why it's becoming more common to see animated neon signs and traveling billboards.

This gentleman was so talented he never slowed down to let people read his message. He simply wanted to perform. Do you do this?

I once assisted with a city tour while working for a convention and visitor bureau. A very important retired military personnel association was considering our destination for its annual convention. During a tour of the first hotel, the new sales manager insisted upon showing the client a brand new racquetball court. She spent more than 20 minutes pointing out every detail from the type of wood on the floor to the thickness of the glass wall. The group was short on time and never had a chance to view the ballroom, which was the most important part of the property for them to see. The sales manager lost the business and the association chose another hotel.

This salesperson was so focused on "performing" that he totally ignored the customer's needs.

Motion may attract attention but it doesn't attract business.

MPD: Deliver information that is
needed, not just what you
want to talk about.

Strategies For Sales Activities And Shoveling Snow

In 2009, Washington, D.C. was hit with one of the most substantial snowstorms in recent history.

More than two feet of snow fell near my home by Dulles International Airport.

The snow was rapidly accumulating and I had to make a decision. Do I sled with the kids and drink hot chocolate with the family or do I begin to shovel? Pushing heavy snow around is never fun but having a clean driveway is always helpful.

Crazy as it sounds I thought about sales activities while shoveling. Maintaining a record of sales activities isn't always fun but it's a critical part of the job. Do you let the paperwork accumulate or do you have a firm handle on your daily activities?

I decided to keep up with "my activities" (shoveling snow) as the snow fell. And I quickly realized I could handle a manageable load of snow. If I waited any longer the snow would've been that much heavier to lift.

Do you keep track of your tax documents and receipts throughout the year or do you scramble to find your paperwork right before tax day?

If you shovel when it snows and if you document sales activities as they occur… Your tasks will be evenly distributed and you'll be able to achieve the same results with less effort!

MPD: Keep up with your
administrative duties.

Tell Me A Story

You and your team members should always find ways to differentiate yourselves from the competition. Customers often try to push suppliers into a "transactional" mode and may base their decisions on price alone. I like to encourage salespeople to stress the value of successful meetings to their clients. Just about every hotel has flat-screen televisions these days but how many hotels have a housekeeper who hasn't missed a day of work in 27 years? She knows her frequent guests by name, remembers their preferences and continues to smile despite her two-hour commute.

A local restaurant advertised a $75 per couple package that included limousine transportation and dinner for two with a bottle of wine. I never would have considered this restaurant before reading the ad in the Sunday paper. My philosophy is I can always afford $75 if it creates a good experience.

The biggest challenge for any company is to identify the items that make your business different and unique. What separates you from the competition? If you can't compete on features alone (there will always be a newer product or service in your marketplace), what are the intangible items that will lead customers your way?

The same lesson applies to candidates who are trying to differentiate themselves during a job interview. What separates you from all the other applicants? Can you adequately and eloquently describe what makes you unique?

Tell me a story...

MPD: Tell stories to create differentiation.

Big Houses, Big Mailboxes, Big Bills

My family and I once walked through a luxurious neighborhood adjacent to Trump National Golf Club in Virginia. One interesting thing we noticed was that each of the large homes came with a gigantic mailbox (about four times the normal size). My kids asked me about this and the only reasonable explanation I could provide was that "big homes" come with "big bills."

Years ago one of my sales managers wanted to learn more about leading a team. I encouraged her but also reminded her that more responsibilities (and often pressure) are associated with director titles. I concur that each of us wants to progress in our respective careers. However, we also need to be reminded of the responsibilities that come with new positions. Don't be clouded by the excitement that a new position brings without understanding all aspects. I recently met a former vice president of sales who returned to a property as a bellman. Our neighbors are moving out of their 4,000-square-foot home into a two-bedroom condo to simplify their lives.

One of my mentors made a decision early in his career to accept positions that would require him to spend significant amounts of time away from his family. I turned down a terrific position that would've moved my family thousands of miles away from my sick mother-in-law.

What type of mailbox are you looking for?

MPD: Seek to understand the pros and the cons of any new opportunity.

Bart Berkey

Follow Up

I researched a new Infiniti car for about three months and finally found one close to our home. It wasn't my first choice but I thought I would settle at a fair price and buy it.

I started with a test drive at dealership A. I could tell the salesman already felt he had the sale in the bag. Keep in mind all our previous communication occurred via e-mail. He made no attempt to get to know me. "Why was I looking for a new car?" "What kind of color do I want?" NOTHING.

So I decided to visit dealership B.

They didn't have my preferred color combination but the salesman made an effort to stay in touch and gauge my flexibility. He got to know my preferences and me. He called a few days later to say he found my desired color combination and would sell the car at a price slightly lower than dealership A.

When I picked up the car the general manager introduced himself. The salesman was kind, sincere and gracious. The finance person tried to build a rapport even though the sale was essentially done. The general manager even sent me a photo of my new car while I was completing the paperwork.

Don't assume a sale is ever final until it's final. I'm enjoying my new car and would recommend dealership B to anyone.

MPD: Keep building relationships even after the deal is done.

The Importance Of Taking Notes

How is your memory? Can you remember the smallest details?

"I trust the weakest pen more than the strongest memory."

– Tim Ferriss

I was conducting one of our weekly sales meetings and noticed that several team members didn't bring anything with them to the meeting. So I chose to play a game to inspire some learning.

"Take out a piece of paper and write the word 'hotel' on it," I said. "Now see how many different words you can create by using the letters from the word 'hotel'."

Anyone who identified more than five words could leave the office early that day.

Can you guess what happened to those people who didn't bring anything to the meeting? Some borrowed scraps of paper from their colleagues but most couldn't even find a pen.

More importantly, everyone came prepared with a pen and notebook the following week.

Taking notes shows respect.

Note-taking might not be as important to us as it is for doctors. But this practice might remind you to remove all Pepsi products from the mini bar for the executive directors attending a Coca-Cola conference. It can also guarantee that you correctly spell the names of your customer's children for their personalized amenities.

Name the author I just referenced in the first paragraph.

If only you had been taking notes.

MPD: Take notes to show respect and remember details.

Bart Berkey

How To Hustle; Tips From A Trash Collector

Have you ever left your home in the early morning to nearly miss hitting a garbage truck? I recently witnessed the extreme focus and hustle exerted by our local trash collectors. They were running from house to house in a full-out sprint. I wondered why and did some research on the Internet.

It turns out collectors start early to avoid causing traffic delays for commuters with their constant stops. This also allows them to take the trash to the landfills before they close.

Waste management employees (who run an average of 20 miles per day) are also able to get a full day's pay no matter how early they finish their routes.

If only that "hustle" could be balanced with a little "carefulness" to prevent damage to trash cans...

MPD: Motivate your employees to accomplish their goals early.

Today I Walked Only One Dog

Many of my stories and life lessons center around my dogs. Our prince, Bruno, passed away recently from internal complications. Only a few hours elapsed from the time my wife called me to the time the kids kissed him goodbye. He was a wonderful companion and a perfect pet.

Here are a few of his greatest qualities:

- Bruno never complained
- He was up for anything and everything
- He did not ask for much but he returned plenty
- He was happy, he communicated and he showed appreciation
- He was patient and he didn't cry

We cried.

I hope others can experience the same companionship. Bruno was part of the family but he was also a great employee in a sense. He worked for us by greeting us warmly, by giving us attention when we needed it, and by catching a ball upon request to take the cares of the day away.

May you find perfection in all your pets and employees.

MPD: Appreciate great friends,
whether two or four-legged.

Top 3 Reasons To Connect On LinkedIn

I just returned from a college event where I encouraged all the students I met to join LinkedIn. One student said he wouldn't have enough time to complete a profile because he focused all his attention on Facebook.

Here's why it might make sense for this senior to be connected to alumni and other contacts:

I received a message from a recruiter who was searching for recent college graduates with an interest in entry-level hospitality sales programs. The positions offered a base salary of $60,000 and the candidates could work from anywhere in the country.

Reason #1: You're looking for a job.

I sent the request to a student who just accepted a different position; he forwarded it (via LinkedIn) to a friend.

Reason #2: You know someone who's looking for a job.

A second student applied and also shared the information with a fraternity brother who wasn't enjoying his job. The fraternity brother accepted the position!

Reason #3: You would like to grow personally for yourself and professionally for your company.

Staying connected is good for business but it also helps to build and maintain relationships with friends and colleagues. Isn't this the reason we got into this industry in the first place?

I personally invite you to connect with me on LinkedIn and I will graciously accept. My motivation falls into "Reason #3" and perhaps one of my 3,000+ contacts can assist you in the future!

MPD: Use LinkedIn extensively.

---

7 Ways To Retain Your Best Employees

I had the pleasure of participating in a meeting with 17 senior sales leaders from the top domestic hotel management companies. These leaders together represented more than 800 properties. As business improves, the focus shifts to recruiting and retaining the best employees. Below is a summary of the revelations from our conversation:

Top Ways to Keep the Best Employees and Salespeople (for organizations and senior leaders to consider):

1. Respect your team (like you would a customer)
2. Develop personal relationships, and care for your employees and their careers
3. Establish monthly recognition programs
4. Ensure that veteran salaries are equitable when bringing in new talent at high salary levels; Increase veteran's wages at appropriate levels above newly hired, less experienced talent
5. Eliminate obstacles
6. Offer flexibility with lifestyle needs (work at home, job share, etc.)
7. Show appreciation to the families of team members for their contributions and dedication to the company and to their jobs

We also discussed why employees might leave their jobs.

Top Reasons Employees Leave Jobs:

1. Growth opportunities outside current organization (i.e. moving from a smaller hotel to a larger non-managed hotel in the same city)
2. Performance evaluations (if salespeople aren't able to keep up with revenue requirements)
3. Client steals them away
4. Recent college graduates don't like the industry
5. Individuals leaving for higher paying jobs
6. Following friends and bosses who leave

MPD: Sincerely care.

Tried And True

Many people can feel intimidated entering the workforce for the first time. Expectations set by bosses and supervisors vary from those set by professors and parents. There are no "dog ate my homework" excuses in the real world and no opportunities to run home to mom and dad for a home-cooked meal.

Our education system prepares us to be organized, meet deadlines and accept responsibilities. These tasks are undoubtedly very important but also need to be combined with real-world expertise. "Work smarter, not harder" is a statement said by many but applied by very few.

I was in high school when my sister invited me to visit her at the Pittsburgh Convention and Visitor's Bureau. She introduced me to the president who shared the following advice:

1. Always dress like you're interviewing for a million dollar job
2. Always follow up to show your appreciation
3. Always come prepared with meaningful questions

Few people have access to the president of a company for advice or a mentor who provides real-life suggestions. It seems like only yesterday when I took my first step into corporate life. I'm hopeful you can learn from my experiences without enduring some of the struggles I encountered navigating through the real world. The lessons I learned have been <u>tried</u> as I personally experienced them, and <u>true</u> as they've enabled me to learn more about happiness and success.

MPD: Listen to the advice of successful individuals.

Update Your Resume This Weekend

Do you have plans this weekend? Will you spend hours watching a sporting event or a movie? Consider dedicating an hour to work on your career by updating your resume.

In advance of a college recruitment trip, I collected 31 student resumes from graduating seniors who wanted to speak with me. I didn't have enough time to meet all the candidates and had to narrow down my top choices to only five. As I reviewed each resume it became clear who showed the greatest potential.

Here are a few suggestions for those looking to improve the influence of their resume:
- Keep resumes well organized in a simple format without typographical errors. I was amazed at how many people didn't spell check their documents.
- List experiences that are relevant to the field you're pursuing. Someone who wants to get into a "rooms training program" should have experience at the front desk or in housekeeping. It may be easy to work for the same restaurant every summer but serious people know this is not what "summers are made for."

"A ship in a harbor is safe, but that's not what ships were meant for."
– William Shedd

- Show accomplishments for each job and not just duties. A resume should not be a job description with your name on it. Give details and metrics (i.e. increased customer satisfaction by 27% in a three month period).
- Are you a leader or a follower? Obtain leadership roles within your organizations.
- Be proud of your accomplishments and awards. List them. What makes you different?
- What have you done to give back to the community? Are your actions aimed at helping others?

Once you update your resume be sure to enhance your online profiles with the same information (i.e. LinkedIn) so they're current and powerful.

MPD: Improve your resume.

What You Achieved, Not What You Did

A friend and former colleague wanted to return to the hospitality industry after a two-year break. She shared her resume with me but it didn't read nearly as well as it should. A common mistake I find with many resumes (going back to my recruiter days) is that most people list their day-to-day responsibilities and forget to include their accomplishments.

I presented to a group of college students recently that wanted to apply their hospitality degrees to the food and beverage/restaurant side of the industry. I asked the group these questions:
- "Who has worked in a restaurant before?" 8 out of 20 students raised their hands.
- "Who has held the position of server?" 6 out of the 8 raised their hands.
- "Tell me about your experience as a server as I can only hire one of you."

Five students talked about taking orders, providing good service, clearing dishes and mastering the menu. There was one student who stood out above the others:

"After three months I showed enough leadership to be promoted to the official trainer for the wait staff. Many servers had been at the restaurant longer than me so I needed to approach the situation delicately. We collectively developed a team approach and formulated a training program for all new employees. I increased the average check for my customers by 28 percent by developing a dessert upsell program and rolled out the program to the other team members."

Who would you hire? Are you simply doing your job? Can you do your job better by focusing on accomplishments? Keeping track of your achievements will not only benefit your resume (for job seekers) but will also positively contribute to your year-end review (for those not seeking a new position).

MPD: Focus on achievements.

Why Do You Do This?

You just completed an 18-hour shift. You're too exhausted to sleep and only have enough energy to fill a bowl with milk and cereal. <u>Why do you do this?</u>

There are many other industries that allow you to earn more and work less. <u>Why do you do this?</u>

I've seen many people in our industry sacrifice relationships by uprooting themselves and their families every two years. When the family can't follow they may see their kids every other weekend. Some of my greatest mentors have chosen to be away from families for months at a time to advance their careers.

One summer my family and I went to a county fair that featured a traveling carnival. I struck up a conversation with one of the "carnies" while my kids were throwing darts at balloons. I asked him where he lived and he answered, "Wherever my RV is parked." The night before he treated his wife to a motel stay so she could take a real shower. He complained about the price of gas but other than that he seemed pretty happy. He loved his job and enjoyed traveling the country.

My family is the most important thing in my life. In my recruiting days, I would tell candidates to make decisions that make them happy. Perhaps I chose the sales route so I would work more normal hours than my operational counterparts and have weekends off.

Steve Pavlina is an entrepreneur who challenged individuals to discover their purpose in life by writing down the first ideas that came to mind when they asked themselves that question. The answers that make you cry define your purpose. I believe family and making others feel comfortable combine to create my purpose.

I continue to learn about things that make others tick. I try to incorporate other people's passions into my own to create a greater knowledge of myself.

Why do you do this or why are you going to do this?

MPD: Discover your passion and purpose.

The Truth About Your Life In Sales

Years ago I received an e-mail from Dickinson + Associates, a management consulting firm based in Chicago. I felt the message was meaningful enough to save and put in a protective sheet to keep with my favorite sales thoughts.

It states, "Stop asking great questions and start being interested. A sales meeting isn't the invasion of Normandy. Stop overthinking and over planning the conversation. Humans want to be heard and understood. They want to be appreciated and to feel interesting and wise. The very best salespeople are those who bring a warm curiosity to the meeting. They delight in learning and they listen to understand."

In today's business world it's not enough to be a good salesperson. You have to position yourself differently from the competition. The difference may not be how your meeting space compares to your competition. It could be your ability as a salesperson.

I love asking questions. I want to learn what makes other people tick. I ask questions because I'm sincerely interested in listening. Perhaps I can appreciate the joy others find in their lives and can incorporate that happiness into mine.

Not a bad way to approach sales; enhance your life and obtain revenue!

MPD: Be interesting and genuinely curious.

Owning The Attitude I Should've Rented

Too big for your britches? Do you think you're more important than you really are? What are you doing every day to prove your worth?

There are certain jobs – including sales – that require results every day. Other positions may only require weekly or monthly goals. A celebrity said in a radio interview that he spent his entire paycheck on a sports car after landing his first acting job. Three years went by before he found another paying gig. In hindsight, he realized he "should've rented the attitude instead of owning it" since his fame was only temporary.

I see the same attitude exhibited by professionals when they reach a particular level. They'll look you in the eyes and pretend to listen until someone more important comes along. I'm extremely sensitive to this and always try my best to look everyone in the eyes. Make them feel as if listening to them is the most important thing you should be doing. I notice salespeople will look at name badges during tradeshow events even before looking at faces. People are people. Treat everyone with respect.

I interviewed a gentleman who lost his job after being mean to his employees, several of whom were my friends. He was arrogant, cruel and aloof. He contacted me after he was fired and approached me for a job. I was professional during the interview process and asked about his experiences, but couldn't shake his negative reputation from my mind. We continued the search and found a person who was a better "fit" for the role. If only he had "rented" the attitude he chose to "own" so he could've positively impacted the lives of those who worked for him.

MPD: Remain grounded despite the height of your awards and level of your position.

Consequences

How can you motivate yourself to accomplish things when there is no consequence of laziness? You may hear stories of people who think it's easier to collect an unemployment check than to put forth the effort to find a job.

An overweight man may not start an exercise program and revise his eating habits until he's at risk of diabetes or heart disease. A college student may refrain from searching for a job when it's comfortable, easy, and free to live at home after graduation. She may not act until she's faced with the reality of paying rent and handling her own expenses. A lazy husband may not clean the house for a dinner party until his work friends are invited for a celebration. A business may not place sandbags by the front doors during hurricane season until the first few drops of rain begin to fall.

Truly successful people are those who have discipline and perseverance. They get things done not because of the consequences of inaction but because they feel a sense of accomplishment when something is complete.

When you hire new employees be sure to ask, "What motivates you?" Listen intently for the answer and see if the motivation comes intrinsically or extrinsically. Earlier this year I had dinner with a successful restaurateur whose upbringing motivated him to work hard in life. His father said he would never rise to the top. This propelled him to overcome obstacles and work exceptionally hard as an adult. This restaurateur misses his father but continues to push himself everyday. He strives to make a positive impact on his company and the people he leads.

Do you consistently make the extra effort to improve yourself? Do you help make the world a better place because it's the right thing to do? Or do you do these things only when the consequences of "not doing" outweigh the effort needed to accomplish these items?

MPD: Make the effort for the right reasons.

Eat Almonds Not Cashews

Last year I asked my nutritionist to run a blood test since my cholesterol and sugar levels were exceptionally high. I went on a strict diet, eliminated almost all sugar and dairy, ate more vegetables and fish, and reduced my red meat and alcohol intake.

After six months my numbers drastically improved. I didn't need any additional medicine and my nutritionist said I was no longer at risk of developing diabetes. I lost 30 pounds and reached my lowest weight since college. I was energized and enthused. I could no longer see my "double chin" in the reflection from my iPad.

Time passed and I remember going to a relative's birthday party. Everyone ate steak and I had chicken. They ate Chinese food and I had a salad. They finished with a brownie and I only had a small bite. My body no longer craved sugar and carbohydrates.

I thought I had this new lifestyle under control. So I decided to have two bites of cake instead of one. I had two glasses of wine instead of a sip. I ate cashews instead of the almonds that were prescribed for my diet.

A second visit to the doctor revealed that my numbers were approaching the same high levels from before. I missed the way I felt when I had healthier eating habits. I missed the way my clothes would fit and the way I looked in photographs. Today, I'm strict with my diet and exercise again.

A professional athlete trains year round. A professional corporate athlete also needs to train year round. What are the commitments you're making to yourself personally and professionally? Are you able to find a balance between your personal and professional life? What types of commitments are you making to your customers?

"I'm leaving the office early today and can't respond to your lead."
"I'm on vacation next week and will reply when I return."
Are you going to eat healthy before you put on a bathing suit or go for your next blood test?

Today, eat almonds and not cashews.

MPD: Commit to find balance and happiness.

Bart Berkey

My Dry Cleaner Wears Wrinkled Shirts

Do you "walk the walk" and "talk the talk?"

When I picked up my dry cleaning the other day, I realized that the owner always dresses impeccably well and looks neatly pressed. It's what I expect and one of the reasons why I give him my business. The employees built my trust simply by their appearance and their actions.

How would you feel if your dry cleaner looked like a wrinkled mess?

What if your dentist had crooked teeth and your dermatologist had blemishes? How would you react if an entomologist stepped on a bug during a tour of the zoo's insect house?

Do you provide outstanding service at all times? I hear stories of colleagues who always open doors for people. Others pick up trash in hotel lobbies when they're off the clock. This chapter is a tribute to you as service professionals and the ways you make this world a better place.

MPD: Exude respectability inside and outside the workplace.

A Tale Of The Eggs Rock And Finding Your Purpose

In Sintra, Portugal there is a tall rock with yellow markings that sits high above the rest of the landscape. It's a beautiful site and local legend tells the story of how the rock received such colorful yellow stains. Under the stone, as the folklore goes, sat a hidden magic treasure that could be retrieved by anyone who moved the massive rock. An old lady from the nearby village grew up wanting to become a queen. She planned on fulfilling her wish as soon as she moved the rock and uncovered the hidden treasure.

Each day she would carry a huge basket of eggs and hike up the mountain to the rock. She would hurl the eggs one at a time to try and dislodge the rock to reveal the treasure. She continued this ritual everyday until she died.

Many say the woman's attitude changed from negative to positive the day she identified this new task and purpose. The hike combined with the relaxing views from the top of the mountain helped to essentially double her life. She never became a queen but enriched her life with this challenge.

What is your purpose and is it helping you to live a long, fulfilled life?

Is your job sucking the life out of you and prohibiting you to live your life?

MPD: Find your purpose to enrich
your life.

Bart Berkey

About the Author

Most People Don't watch others to see what makes them successful, nor do they incorporate these qualities into their own lives to enrich themselves.

Most People Don't direct their efforts toward self-improvement.

Most People Don't try to change things they dislike. For the past 24 years, Bart has been able to achieve happiness and success by applying the lessons of others into his own personal life.

From years as a recruiter selecting "the best of the best", to leading part of a domestic global sales team for a highly respected luxury organization, Bart has made a tremendous impact on thousands of individuals. He was recognized as one of the "Top 25 Most Extraordinary Minds in Sales and Marketing" and continues to energize and inspire others through his life coaching, written works, and speaking engagements.

After graduating from Penn State University, Bart started his career with Hyatt Hotels and Resorts in various on property and corporate positions. He earned "Manager of the Year" before being recruited to join StarCite as their Vice President of Sales. After several years in the meetings technology field, he broadened his experience by serving as Regional Vice President for the Long Beach Convention and Visitors Bureau, before heading up the Washington, DC office for the St. Louis Convention and Visitors Commission. His current role (Senior Corporate Director, Eastern Region Global Sales Office with a luxury hotel company) allows him to lead a sales team that represents the entire brand portfolio to a selection of their top group and business travel customers. He is passionate about his family and helping others.

Bart lives in the Washington, DC area with his wife and two children.

MPD: Network with Bart on Linkedin.com.

MPD: Stay connected with Bart

Bart's inspirational message is available to be delivered in person to your group or organization. To learn more about all the exciting programs Bart has to offer:

E-mail: bartberkey@gmail.com
Twitter: @bartberkey
Website: www.bartberkey.net

To order additional copies of this book and to review his website, please visit:

www.bartberkey.net

CPSIA information can be obtained at www.ICGtesting.com
Printed in the USA
BVOW06s0843191115

427556BV00002B/2/P